WOMEN IN SOCIETY

UNITED STATES OF AMERICA

PENNY COLMAN

MARSHALL CAVENDISH
New York • London • Sydney

Reference edition published 1994 by
Marshall Cavendish Corporation
2415 Jerusalem Avenue
P.O. Box 587
North Bellmore
New York 11710

© Times Editions Pte Ltd 1994

Originated and designed by
Times Books International, an imprint of
Times Editions Pte Ltd

Printed in Malaysia

Library of Congress Cataloging-in-Publication Data:
Colman, Penny.
    Women in society. United States / Penny Colman.
      p. cm.
    Age level: 10–14: grade level: 5 and up.
    Includes bibliographical references (p.   ) and index.
    ISBN 1-85435-559-7 (set). — ISBN 1-85435-560-0
    1. Women—United States—Social conditions—Juvenile
literature. (1. Women—United States. 2. United States—
Social conditions.)
I. Title.
HQ1410.C6 1994
305.42'0973—dc20   93–48706
                        CIP
                        AC

Women in Society

Editorial Director	Shirley Hew
Managing Editor	Shova Loh
Editors	Michael Spilling
	Falak Kagda
	Roseline Lum
	Sue Sismondo
	MaryLee Knowlton
Picture Editor	Penny Colman
	Mee-Yee Lee
Production	Edmund Lam
Design	Tuck Loong
	Ronn Yeo
	Felicia Wong
	Loo Chuan Ming
Illustrators	Anuar bin Abdul Rahim
	Eric Chew
	Atanu Roy
	William Sim
MCC Editorial Director	Evelyn M. Fazio
MCC Production Manager	Ruth Toda

Introduction

The United States of America is a country of ideals and promises. The ideals of liberty and justice. The promises of democracy and economic opportunity. It is a country founded on the Declaration of Independence, a document that includes the words, "We hold these truths to be self-evident, that all men are created equal, that they are endowed by their Creator with certain unalienable rights, that among these are life, liberty, and the pursuit of happiness."

Seen through the eyes of men, these ideals and promises have provided unprecedented opportunity. For women, the opportunities have been limited by obstacles such as laws that prevented them from owning property and by dominant cultural attitudes that value marriage and motherhood above education and economic self-sufficiency. And by the fact that for 133 years after the U.S. Constitution was adopted, women were denied their right to vote.

The story of women in the United States has been distorted in the culture and left out of the history books. But it is there in diaries, letters, court records, books, and oral histories. It is the story of women's efforts to make the rhetoric of the Declaration of Independence and the Constitution reality. It is the story of determined, creative, and courageous women overcoming obstacles, changing laws, and redefining cultural attitudes. It is the story of mothers, teachers, wives, reformers, laborers, and scientists moving forward in ordinary and extraordinary ways to meet the challenges of everyday life and create the future.

Contents

Harriet Tubman

Slave girl Araminta was born in 1820 or 1821, on a plantation in Maryland. The owner of the plantation was Edward Brodas. He provided his slaves with a small cabin, a blanket, a few clothes, a meager supply of food, and demanded that they work hard all day. If they protested, Brodas had them whipped.

Araminta grew up to be a powerful woman known as Harriet Tubman. She was strong and hard-working. About five feet tall, she had formidable features—heavy-lidded, wide-set, dark eyes, strong cheekbones and forehead, a firm mouth with a full lower lip, and well-defined ears. She wore a bandanna wrapped around her head that covered a dent that was put there by a slave overseer when Tubman was trying to protect a runaway slave.

The runaway slave

At the end of a long, hard day of work, one of the slaves slipped away. But the overseer saw him. The slave ran into a store and the overseer cornered him. Ordering Tubman and the other slaves to tie him up, the overseer prepared to whip him. Tubman refused, and the runaway slave jumped up and ran out. The enraged overseer picked up a two-pound weight and threw it at the slave. He missed and hit Harriet Tubman. Her head cracked open, blood gushed out, and she collapsed in a heap.

For the rest of her life, Tubman suffered from severe headaches and seizures that caused her to suddenly fall asleep in the middle of whatever she was doing. After a short time, she would wake up and go on as if nothing had happened.

Opposite: Harriet Tubman's strong personality is evident in this painting by Robert S. Pious.

Right: As a conductor on the Underground Railroad, Harriet Tubman helped many slaves to freedom.

The Underground Railroad

A secret network of people, the Underground Railroad helped escaping slaves reach freedom in the Northern States or Canada. For about 10 years, Harriet Tubman led slaves to freedom. Despite the danger of being captured herself, she slipped back into slave territory about 19 times and brought more than 300 slaves to freedom. She was so effective that the state of Maryland offered a huge reward for her capture. She was called Moses, after the prophet in the Bible who led his people out of slavery in Egypt. A plaque put up in her memory by the city of Auburn, New York, quotes her as saying, "On my Underground Railroad I nebber ran my train off de track an' I nebber los' a passenger."

"Like in heaven"

When she was about 29 years old, Harriet Tubman escaped from slavery. Years later she recalled her reaction when she crossed the border into Pennsylvania, a state that forbid slavery: "…I looked at my hands to see if I was the same person. There was such a glory over everything; the sun came like gold through the trees, and over the fields, and I felt like I was in heaven."

Determined to rescue her family and friends, Tubman became a conductor on the Underground Railroad, and successfully helped hundreds of slaves to freedom.

Called General Tubman, she was tough and resourceful. When one escaping slave lost his nerve and wanted to quit, Tubman aimed her pistol at his head and said, "Move or die!" Once, when she heard a group of men talking about capturing her, Tubman pretended to read a book that she carried, hoping that she had it right side up. Remarking that the Harriet Tubman they were looking for could not read or write, the men ignored her.

Spy commander

Abolitionists had been trying to stop slavery for years. In 1860, Abraham Lincoln was elected president. Eleven Southern states withdrew from the United States. Determined to preserve the United States, Lincoln called up an army of Union troops from the Northern States. On April 12, 1861, shots were fired between northern and southern troops and the Civil War began.

Harriet Tubman did not hesitate to get involved. First she probably went to Maryland and Virginia to help contraband (fugitive) slaves who came to the Union Army for protection. Then she went to South Carolina where she devoted herself to nursing contraband and Union soldiers. Famous for the remedies she prepared, Tubman saved the lives of many sick people.

Before long, Harriet Tubman organized a unit of scouts and spies to operate from South Carolina to Florida. With herself as commander, Tubman handpicked nine black scouts and river pilots. They made repeated trips up the rivers and into the swamps, marshes, and jungles to obtain information about Southern troop strength and defenses. They also surveyed plantations and Southern towns looking for slaves they could enlist in the Northern army.

On June 2, 1863, Harriet Tubman and Colonel James Montgomery conducted one of the most successful raids up the Combahee River. They captured enemy supplies and freed many slaves. After the raid, Montgomery and Tubman spoke at a celebration. According to a newspaper reporter, "The Colonel was followed by a speech from the black woman, who led the raid and under whose inspiration it was originated and conducted. For sound sense and real native eloquence, her address would do honor to any man, and it created a great sensation…"

Helping her people

The Civil War ended in 1865. Harriet Tubman spent the rest of her life in Auburn, New York. She helped former slaves start a new life, spoke out about women's rights, and founded a cooperative farm and home for the poor, sick, and homeless black people.

On March 10, 1913, surrounded by friends, Harriet Tubman died. A spruce tree was planted over her grave. Today it is a magnificent tree—tall and straight with dark green needles and long cones on swooping branches that shelter Tubman's grave and taper to a point high above the site.

Harriet Tubman dedicated herself to the fight for freedom.

chapter two

Milestones

Just over 200 years old, the United States of America is a young country, but people have been living on the land for thousands of years. The first people, known as Paleo-Indians, came from Asia about 20,000 or even 40,000 years ago across a land bridge that is now covered by the Bering Strait. The Paleo-Indians were hunters, and they followed huge animals—giant bisons, woolly mammoths, and caribou—to a land where no people had lived before. Living as nomads, the Paleo-Indians traveled in small family bands and eventually spread from the Arctic to the southernmost tip of South America. Some Paleo-Indians supplemented hunting with gathering seeds, roots, and fruit. The earliest known remains of ancient people in America are those of a woman who was buried in Colorado 9,000 years ago.

About 6,000 years ago, the people who lived in what is now Mexico figured out how to grow crops of corn, beans, and squash. In time, this knowledge spread northward to the people living in what is now the United States, who are ancestors of contemporary Native Americans—the Cherokee, Cheyenne, Pueblo, Nez Percé, Seminole, Mohegan, Apache. With the knowledge of agriculture in addition to hunting, fishing, and gathering, a great diversity of Native American cultures developed. Although the societies were very different from each other, they had common features such as traditions of story-telling and religion and were built around families and clans. And, in every society, women played important roles.

Opposite: Mary Tippee was one of the women who followed the Collis Zouaves, a volunteer regiment from Pennsylvania, during the American Civil War.

Right: Basket-weaving is a traditional occupation among Hopi women.

Chronology

40,000 B.C.	People living in North America.
A.D. 1014	The last Scandinavian expedition to the Americas is commanded by a woman, Freydis Ericson.
1492	Christopher Columbus lands in the Bahamas.
1565	Spanish and Portuguese women settle in St. Augustine, Florida, the first U.S. permanent settlement.
1587	Virginia Dare, first English child born in America.
1609	120 women and children arrive in Jamestown, Virginia, the first permanent English settlement in North America.
1619	First Africans brought to America and sold to settlers in Virginia. By 1660, about one-third of all African slaves are women.
	London merchants send two boatloads of English woman as prospective wives for settlers in Jamestown, Virginia.
1765–1769	Sir William Blackstone, an English jurist, writes in the Commentaries on the Laws of England: "By marriage, the husband and wife are one person in the law...the very being and legal existence of the woman is suspended during the marriage, or at least is incorporated into that of her husband under whose wing (and) protection she performs everything."
1777–1807	All states pass laws which deny women suffrage.
1833	Oberlin College, the first to accept students regardless of race or sex, established.
1848	The First Woman's Rights Convention held in the United States. Participants sign the Declaration of Sentiments with a list of resolutions to end discrimination against women.
1868	Fourteenth Amendment added to the U.S. Constitution: the word "male" is used to describe a "citizen."
1869	Wyoming Territory grants suffrage for men and women. It becomes a state in 1890.
1916	Jeannette Rankin from Montana, first woman elected to the U.S. House of Representatives.

1916	Margaret Sanger opens the first birth-control clinic in the United States. She is arrested.
1920	After a long and intense effort, the Nineteenth Amendment to the U.S. Constitution is ratified. It reads: "The right of citizens of the United States to vote shall not be denied or abridged by the United States or by any State on account of sex." Native Americans—male or female—still do not have suffrage. It is granted in 1924 by an act of Congress.
1923	Equal Rights Amendment (ERA) first introduced in Congress. It reads: "Men and women shall have equal rights throughout the United States and in every place subject to its jurisdiction. Congress shall have power to enforce this article by appropriate legislation."
1933	Frances Perkins appointed secretary of labor, the first woman U.S. cabinet member.
1961	President's Commission on the Status of Woman established by President John F. Kennedy.
1963	*The Feminine Mystique* published, a book that launches the modern U.S. women's movement.
1964	Congress passes the Civil Rights Act; one section prohibits employment discrimination on basis of race, color, religion, sex, or national origin.
1966	National Organization for Women organized to work for women's rights.
1972	Congress passes Title IX of Educational Amendments, which makes it illegal for most public schools that receive federal monies to discriminate on the basis of sex. Congress passes the ERA and sends it to the states for ratification. It now reads: "Equality of rights under the law shall not be denied or abridged by the United States or by any state on account of sex."
1982	Time runs out. With just three states short of the number required for ratification, the ERA fails to become part of the U.S. Constitution.
1984	Geraldine Ferraro, first woman nominated by a major political party to run for vice-president of the United States.
1993	ERA reintroduced in Congress. The drive continues to get it passed and ratified.

Native American women

According to a legend told by the Iroquois people, in the beginning there was nothing but water where various water animals and birds lived. Then one day a woman fell out of the heavens. Seeing her fall, two loons flew under her and held her up with their bodies. The loons' call attracted other creatures to the scene. As the loons were tiring, the tortoise offered to hold the woman. That's how the tortoise's back became the land, and the woman lived there. In time she gave birth to three children. Her sons were disagreeable and quarreled with each other, which can still be heard in the thunder. Her daughter became the mother of the great Iroquois Nation.

There are many Native American myths, legends, and stories with women as the central figure. They reflect women's indispensable roles in Native American societies. Women fulfilled essential responsibilities—caring for the children; gathering seeds, roots, and fruit; planting and harvesting crops; making household utensils and furnishings; building dwellings; and preserving and preparing food. In hunting societies, women processed the hides of animals and turned them into clothing, blankets, and tepees. Women were also religious leaders and healers.

Native American women prepared the animal hide used to build the tepee in the background.

Pocahontas

Probably because the history of the United States was mostly written by white men, Pocahontas (1595?–1617) is the most well-known Native American woman in U.S. history. Why? Because she saved the life of a white man. At least, that is what the man claimed. The man was Captain John Smith, leader of the first settlers in Jamestown, Virginia.

Pocahontas was the daughter of Chief Powhatan ("POW-uh-TAN"). Powhatan was the ruler of the more than 200 Native American tribes that were living in the area where the English arrived in 1607 to start what would become the first permanent English settlement in North America. At first Powhatan was friendly toward the English, but due to the increasing demands of the invaders, he became less friendly.

In 1613, the English wanted to force Powhatan to return weapons and Englishmen he had captured, so they kidnapped his daughter Pocahontas. After a year in captivity, Pocahontas married an Englishman, John Rolfe, the first Anglo-Indian marriage in Virginia. Converting to Christianity, Pocahontas took the name Rebecca. In 1616, with her husband and baby, she went to England. As Rebecca and wearing European clothing, Pocahontas was treated like royalty. However, after catching smallpox, she died within a year.

Before Pocahontas's death, John Smith had written a book about America, with no mention of Pocahontas at all. But, after her death, he revised his book and included a story about an incident in which Pocahontas saved his life. Powhatan was about to kill him with a stone war club, but Pocahontas placed her head upon Smith's and begged her father not to kill him. Smith's story about how Pocahontas saved his life has endured in popular culture and many U.S. history books.

Older women wielded considerable influence on Native American communities.

Women's influence In many Native American societies, women had a great deal of influence and power. In the Iroquois Nation, women owned farming tools, long houses, and livestock, which were passed from mother to daughter. At the time of marriage, the husband moved into the wife's community and the children became members of the mother's clan. If marital problems arose, the man moved out. Matrons, or older women, were in charge of the distribution of food and other goods. Although the council elders were men, the matrons nominated them and had the right to "knock off the horns" of those who acted improperly or were dishonest, that is remove them from the council.

Five hundred years ago, when the first Europeans arrived, the Native American population in North America was about 10–12 million—the Iroquois

League stretched from the Great Lakes to the Atlantic Ocean, the Algonquin tribes thrived along the East Coast, and the Pueblo civilization flourished in the Southwest. From the Native American societies, the Europeans learned about many things: crops, including corn, cotton, potatoes, squash, beans, and tomatoes; medicines including plants high in vitamin C; technology including how to cure and prepare animal pelts; and ideas including the principle of impeachment and a decision-making process in which each person had an equal voice. For the natives, the contact with Europeans was disastrous. Millions of them died from diseases the Europeans brought—smallpox, measles, mumps, yellow fever, malaria, and chickenpox. They also died in warfare as they fought to preserve their land.

Colonial America

Scandinavian sailors were probably the first people to sail to North America. In A.D. 1000 Leif Ericson, a Norwegian, landed at a place he called Vinland, now known as Newfoundland. In 1014, Ericson's half-sister, Freydis Ericson, commanded the last Scandinavian expedition to Vinland. Almost 500 years later, in 1492, Christopher Columbus, an Italian, made the next recorded voyage to America. Financed by Queen Isabella of Spain, Columbus was searching for a new route to Asia with all its riches. Instead he landed in the Bahamas. Before long, other explorers followed Columbus to the New World. John Cabot led an English expedition. Jacques Cartier led a French expedition. Hernando de Soto led a Spanish expedition, which included one woman. The woman, Francisca Hinestrosa, came with her husband who was a member of de Soto's expedition to Florida in 1539. Henry Hudson led a Dutch expedition.

As the original 13 colonies prospered, more settlers came from all over Europe.

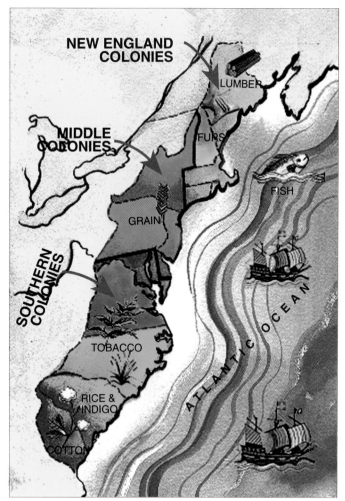

In the late 1500s, the Spanish, French, English, and Dutch made serious attempts at establishing permanent colonies in the New World. By 1630, small settlements stretched along the Atlantic coast. In the early 1700s, growing numbers of immigrants arrived in America. Most of them came from the British Isles. They settled in three areas: the New England Colonies (New Hampshire, Massachusetts, Rhode Island, Connecticut), the Middle Colonies (New York, Pennsylvania, New Jersey, Delaware), and the Southern Colonies (Maryland, Virginia, North Carolina, South Carolina, Georgia). In all 13 colonies, women worked continuously from dawn to sundown. They helped their husbands in the fields while taking care of the household responsibilities. Without their efforts, the colonies would not have survived.

Servants, wives, criminals, and slaves

At first, there were more men than women in America. But, gradually, the number of women increased. They came as indentured servants. They were imported and sold as wives, with their consent, for the price of their voyage. English judges would give women who were convicted of crimes the choice between jail and moving to America. For a time, kidnapping European women for sale in America as indentured servants or wives was a very profitable business. As for African women, there was only one way they came to America—crammed into the holds of ships to be sold as slaves.

Of course, many women chose to come to America. They came with their families in search of a better life. One English minister told his congregation that America had plenty of "berries, minerals, rubies, pearls, gems, grapes, deer, fowl, herbs for food, timber for building, pastures for feeding, and rivers for fishing." They came seeking freedom to practice their religion. They came seeking adventure.

Women slaves had to work just as hard as the men. In addition, they were often sexually abused by their masters.

The Salem Witchcraft Trials

In 1692, several young girls in Danvers, Massachusetts, then called Salem Village, began having mysterious fits of hysteria. After the religious leaders decided that the trouble was caused by witches, the Salem witchcraft trials began. Most of the accused were women. After his wife was accused of being a witch, the governor of Massachusetts finally stopped the trials, but not before 14 women and five men were hanged, an 80-year-old man was tortured to death, and hundreds of people were imprisoned. When Rebecca Nurse, a respectable older woman, dared criticize the trials, she was arrested, hanged, and buried in a common grave with four other victims. Her husband and sons dug up her body secretly and buried it in an unmarked grave near their house.

In 1993, 300 years after the Salem witchcraft trials, a memorial park was dedicated to the victims in Salem. Each victim's name and her or his date of hanging are carved on a stone bench that protrudes from a stone wall. The bench in the picture below commemorates Rebecca Nurse. The flower was placed there by a visitor to the memorial.

Life was hard in America. In early colonial times, perhaps as many as four out of every five women died within five years. Women rarely stopped working. They raised the children, maintained the house and garden, cooked the meals, made the homespun cloth and clothing, soap, candles, preserved foods, tanned leather for shoes, cared for any animals the family owned, and tended to sick or injured people. In addition the women pitched in when extra hands were needed to help plow the fields, clear the forests, or defend against the Native Americans. Women also helped their husbands (printers, innkeepers, silversmiths, and butchers) in their trade. There were also women, especially unmarried women and widows, who ran their own shops, mills, shipyards, and boarding houses. In the 1700s, 16 of the 78 colonial newspapers were printed and published by women.

Inequality Although women and men worked side by side, they did not have the same rights and freedoms. Women could not vote or hold office. Married women could not sign contracts or wills. They did not have the right to their own earnings or property. In fact, a married woman could not act without her husband's approval. While girls were taught domestic skills, they were rarely taught to read and write. Some girls were married by the age of 12 or 13. Single women and widows had more rights and could own property, borrow money, and sue or be sued in court. Women's subordinate position was justified and maintained by two powerful forces: the increasing application of the English Common Law, under which wives had no legal existence apart from their husbands, and the predominance of religions in which women were viewed as obliged to be obedient to men.

Maria Mitchell was one of the few 19th-century women to overcome the obstacles and succeed in the sciences. An astronomer, she discovered a comet.

Born in England, Margaret Brent (c. 1601–c. 1671) moved to America in 1638 and was determined to rise above women's subordinate position. She never married and received the first grant of land made to a woman in the colony of Maryland. A wealthy rancher and money lender, she represented other women in court. As a landowner, she requested the right to vote in the governing body of Maryland, but was refused because she was a woman.

Another woman who was determined to be an independent person was Anne Hutchinson (1591–1643). The first woman to preach to other women, she was jailed, tried, excommunicated, and banished from the Massachusetts Bay Colony for her outspoken views. Known as Mistress Anne, Hutchinson believed that obedience to religious laws was a matter of individual conscience.

Hutchinson arrived in Boston, Massachusetts, in 1634, with her husband and 12 children. Before long, she began holding religious meetings in her home to discuss the male minister's sermon and interpret passages from the Bible. Since, in the Massachusetts Bay Colony, the church and state were considered almost synonymous, Hutchinson's questioning was seen as a great threat to the laws of the government. She was tried by Governor John Winthrop, who had declared her guilty in advance if she did not repudiate her ideas. Hutchinson refused. In 1638,

she was ordered to leave the church and colony forever. Eventually she settled in an area around what is now known as New York City.

The Revolutionary War and the Constitution

The American colonies had strong ties to Britain: most of the colonists came from Britain and they spoke English. Their laws were the same, colonial newspapers printed news about events in Britain, and the British navy and army protected the colonies. People traveled back and forth across the Atlantic Ocean between the colonies and Britain.

Anne Hutchinson was banished from the state of Massachusetts in 1637 because of her religious teachings. A statue of her now stands on the grounds of the State House in Boston, the capital of Massachusetts.

Molly Pitcher played an active part in the War of Independence. This engraving shows her at the Battle of Monmouth.

Eventually, as more immigrants came to America from other countries, the ties between America and Great Britain weakened. People moved farther inland away from the Atlantic Ocean. And, starting in 1765, the British government passed a series of acts to raise money in the colonies. Finally in 1776, the 13 colonies declared their independence from Great Britain. The British government responded with force, and the Revolutionary War began.

Not everybody wanted independence from Great Britain. The patriots did, but not the loyalists. Women were on both sides. Patriot Deborah Sampson Gannett disguised herself as a man and fought in the war. Other women followed the army and carried supplies, cooked meals, and nursed sick and wounded soldiers. As men joined the army, women ran farms and businesses. They rolled bandages, raised money, cut and sewed clothing for the soldiers. They were also spies and messengers.

Because they believed that the British would protect their rights, many Native Americans fought on the side of the British. Those who fought for the Americans included Nanye'hi, "Beloved Woman" of the Cherokee Nation, who warned settlers of attacks. Some 5,000 black Americans fought in the Revolutionary army and navy. By 1781, the British were defeated and surrendered. Two years later, Britain signed a peace treaty and recognized the United States of America as an independent nation.

After the Revolution, many Americans hoped that slavery would end. But it did not. Although many people freed the slaves they owned and a few states made slavery illegal, the slave system in the Southern States continued intact.

"Remember the Ladies" Many people also hoped that women would gain more rights. In 1776, Abigail Adams had even written to her husband John, "In the new Code of Laws which I suppose it would be necessary for you to make I desire you would Remember the Ladies,

> **"Remember all Men would be tyrants if they could. If particular care and attention is not paid to the Ladies we are determined to foment a Rebellion, and will not hold ourselves bound by any Laws in which we have no voice or Representation."**
> —*Abigail Adams to John Adams, March 31, 1776*

and be more generous and favorable to them than your ancestors." In 1787, when John Adams and his colleagues wrote the U.S. Constitution, they did not "remember the ladies." The Revolution did not free women from their legally limited and culturally circumscribed position.

When the U.S. Constitution was written in 1787, no woman was present. It took more than a century for women to gain their constitutional rights.

Above and opposite: Despite the hardships and dangers of the journey, many women did not hesitate to move West with their families.

crops, hunting, fishing, and trading. Other people moved from their farms into towns to work in the newly built factories.

America grew and prospered, and differences in class and status began to appear. There were rich people, poor people, and in between, a rapidly-growing middle class. In addition distinct arenas began to develop for men and women. For men the arena was outside the home where they dealt with politics, business, and money. Women's arena was in the home, and they dealt with home and family. Upper- and middle-class women were expected to exemplify the notion of "true womanhood." They were to be pious, submissive, and devoted to caring for their children and husbands. Working-class women were also expected to be devoted to caring for their children and husband, but they also had to work long hours outside the home for very little money.

The new nation

Dramatic and rapid changes took place in the decades following the Revolution. In 1803, the United States bought the Louisiana Territory, a vast region west of the Mississippi River, from France. This purchase doubled the size of the country. Growing numbers of pioneers moved West to settle in areas far away from the Atlantic Coast. They lived by clearing land, building cabins, growing

The pioneering spirit Between 1840 and 1870, more than a quarter of a million Americans crossed the continental United States. More than 100,000 were women, pioneer women. They gave up the security of family and friendships and headed to unknown lands. With their husbands and children, women traveled by wagons, on horseback, on foot, by steamboat, railroad, and stagecoach. It was a difficult and dangerous journey. But it was also an adventure.

The westward migration had tragic consequences for the Native Americans. They were pushed off their land, and soldiers forced them on long marches to relocate from their homes to strange lands. On a march known as the "Trail of Tears," more than 4,000 Cherokee Indians lost their lives.

Meanwhile, increasing numbers of abolitionists were working to end slavery. They published newspapers, gave speeches, and signed petitions. They also helped runaway slaves escape by moving them along a route from one safe place to another until they reached freedom. This route became known as the Underground Railroad. Women were in the forefront of the abolitionist movement—free black women and white women formed female anti-slavery societies, which were active in every Northern state. Although women were not supposed to speak in public,

> "This is a life I would not exchange for a good deal. There is such independence, so much free air."
> —*Susan Shelby Magoffin, pioneer woman*

that did not stop Angelina and Sarah Grimké, daughters of a wealthy slave owner, and Sojourner Truth, herself a former slave, from speaking out against slavery.

and the bar where men stood to drink. Emma Willard led the effort to provide education for women. Rejecting the prevailing belief that men were intellectually superior to women, Willard started the first all-female school that offered courses such as philosophy, science, and solid geometry. Determined to train women to be teachers, Mary Lyon started the Mount Holyoke Female Seminary, today known as Mount Holyoke College.

A long list of women including Elizabeth Cady Stanton and Susan B. Anthony devoted their lives to fighting for women's rights in the United States.

Women reformers of the 19th century included Elizabeth Cady Stanton *(above, with one of her three children)* and Mary Lyon, whose grave *(right)* stands on the campus of Mount Holyoke College, which she founded.

Women reformers

Throughout the 19th century, women led other reform movements in the United States. Dorothea Lynde Dix conducted a crusade to provide humane care for people with mental illness. Carrie Nation fought against the consumption of alcohol. Carrying an ax and shouting "Smash, women, smash," Nation led her female followers to saloons where they destroyed liquor bottles, glasses, tables, chairs, mirrors,

The Seneca Falls Convention

In 1848, the first women's rights convention was held to discuss the unjust ways women were treated by laws and social customs—a woman could not vote, hold public office, sign a contract, or make a will without her husband's or father's permission. Women had limited rights to own property. In case of divorce, a woman's husband controlled the children.

Considered the beginning of the women's movement in the United States, the convention was held in Seneca Falls, New York. One hundred women and men signed a list of resolutions including a call for woman's suffrage, the right to vote, and a Declaration of Sentiments (engraved on the wall below) that amended the familiar words of the Declaration of Independence to read: "We hold these truths to be self-evident that all men *and women* are created equal."

The Civil War

For years, the issue of slavery had divided the United States. In 1861, when Abraham Lincoln became president, 11 Southern states seceded and formed a new government, the Confederate States of America.

On April 12, 1861, the Civil War began. Women were an integral part of the war on both sides. Elizabeth Van Lew, a passionate abolitionist, was an important Union spy. Rose O'Neal Greenhow was a Confederate spy. Women fought as soldiers. They served as nurses and doctors.

In the North, more than 20,000 volunteer groups of women were formed to raise money and make bandages, uniforms, and blankets. Women also worked in factories, and ran farms and businesses. In the South, women suffered particular hardship because most of the fighting took place there.

Freed black women joined the fight. Harriet Tubman served as a nurse and spy. Susie King Taylor became a nurse and taught black soldiers to read and write. In the South, many slaves escaped. Some joined the army. Others washed clothes, cooked, and nursed. But many died of starvation and disease because there was little food or shelter.

After four years of killing and destruction, the Civil War ended. The Confederacy was defeated and slavery became illegal. The war had a profound impact on many women. Black women were free. Women who had taken over while the men fought gained new skills and self-confidence.

Wounded Union soldiers take a rest in the company of their nurse. Women were particularly active during the Civil War in the medical field and as spies.

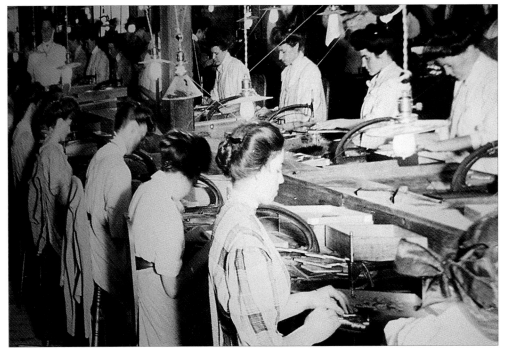

Women workers in a 19th-century factory.

Industrialization and urbanization

Following the Civil War, vast changes took place in the United States as America became the world's leading industrial power. Industrialization created many new jobs for women; backbreaking, low-paying jobs in factories and mills where they worked 12–14 hours a day, six days a week. Many of them were recent immigrants desperate for work. In an effort to improve their situation, many women joined labor unions. Eastern and Midwestern industrial cities expanded rapidly.

In the western half of the country, European-American ranchers, miners, and farmers expanded their settlements. Women worked side-by-side with their husbands, and continued to be fully responsible for raising the children and maintaining the home. Many single and widowed women found work running stores, boarding houses, and laundries. They also could own a section of western land by cultivating it for five years. Western territories and states were the first to grant woman's suffrage.

Women moved very slowly into traditionally male professions. Belva Lockwood became the first woman lawyer to practice before the U.S. Supreme Court. Some women had successful writing careers—Louisa May Alcott, Willa Cather, and Ellen Glasgow. A few women became dentists, scientists, and artists. Most women, however, became teachers and nurses, traditionally female professions with low pay and low status.

THEY RISE OR FALL TOGETHER

It took American women decades of demonstrating, protesting, marching, and picketing before they were finally granted the vote.

World War I In 1917, the United States entered World War I. Like the men who went to fight, the women participated in the war effort. Jobs that had been closed to them were suddenly open—mechanics, munitions workers, truck drivers, police officers, welders. The war ended in 1918 and returning soldiers replaced the women workers.

Finally, woman's suffrage Throughout the war, women continued their drive for woman's suffrage. Women marched, picketed the White House, went to jail,

"It is doubtful if any man...ever realized what the suffrage struggle came to mean to women.... How much of time and patience, how much of work, energy, aspiration, how much of faith, how much of hope, how much of despair went into it. It leaves its mark on one, such a struggle."
—*Carrie Chapman Catt, leader of the drive for woman's suffrage*

undertook hunger strikes, wrote letters, and signed petitions until Congress finally passed the Nineteenth Amendment to the U.S. Constitution, which stated "the right of citizens of the United States to vote shall not be denied by the United States or by any State on account of sex." The amendment was ratified by the states in 1920. Finally, 144 years after the Declaration of Independence, more than half of the U.S. population won the right to vote.

During the 1920s, the country enjoyed great prosperity. Large numbers of cars were produced. So were radios, refrigerators, washing machines, and vacuum cleaners. Electricity became widely used for lighting, cooking, and household appliances. People listened to the radio and went to movies. Through the efforts of Margaret Sanger, information about birth-control devices became available. Increasing numbers of women entered college. Middle-class white women experienced unprecedented freedom, but not for long.

The Great Depression and the New Deal

In 1929, America plunged into an economic crisis—the Great Depression. Millions of people lost their jobs. Black and Mexican-American women who were primarily limited to domestic or agricultural work were particularly hard hit by the Depression. Men were given jobs before married women. Many married women who had jobs were forced to quit. In 1932, Franklin Delano Roosevelt, who pledged to bring a "new deal" to the American people, was elected president. He appointed Frances Perkins as secretary of labor, the first woman cabinet member. Perkins designed major social programs to assist the American people.

Frances Perkins was the first American woman cabinet member.

Women fulfilled many roles during World War II. These three Native American women were Marine Corps reservists.

World War II

In 1941, the United States entered World War II on the side of the Allies. Millions of men went to war in Europe and in the Pacific. In the United States, millions of women went to work. Women did all the jobs left by men: they worked as shipbuilders, welders, and electricians; they built airplanes, drove fire trucks, and assembled bombs. Several hundred thousand women were directly involved in the war: they served in the armed forces as noncombat pilots, nurses, and clerks. Women learned new skills and received high pay. The number of black women workers in factories doubled. Married women got jobs in record numbers. So did women with disabilities.

Postwar America

When the war began, the U.S. government had launched an intensive media campaign to lure women into the labor force. In 1945, the war ended, and the government launched another intensive media campaign to force women out of the labor force. Women were urged to "stay home." A "normal" woman, women were told, devoted herself to her husband and children. She fulfilled herself by baking, cleaning, and keeping herself attractive for her husband. All Americans were urged to consume—to buy new homes, new cars, new electric appliances, televisions, clothes, and cameras. And, Americans did. They also had babies in record numbers. Despite the pressure to stay at home, growing numbers of married women took paid jobs. Other divorced and widowed women provided the primary financial support for their families.

Civil rights movement

Despite slavery having been abolished for more than a century, racial segregation and discrimination was still rampant in the United States. Black children and white children went to separate schools. In the south, there were separate public drinking fountains for blacks and whites, and separate sections in movie theaters. Black people had to ride at the back of the bus. During the 1940s and 1950s, people challenged segregation and discrimination. Many bold and brave black women led the fight—Daisy Bates, Ella Baker, Rosa Parks, and Fannie Lou Hamer. A series of Supreme Court decisions and new laws finally made segregation and discrimination illegal.

After World War II, as the United States became a leader in world politics, many Americans organized and took part in marches and demonstrations for civil rights.

Modern-day women's movement

In 1963, Betty Friedan, a white suburban housewife, wrote a book entitled *The Feminine Mystique.* In it she challenged the notion that women found total fulfillment through childbearing and homemaking. Calling this notion a myth, Friedan charged advertisers, educators, and psychologists with deliberately selling it to women. Friedan's book became a bestseller and launched the modern-day women's movement. Within 10 years, numerous national and grassroots organizations had been formed to promote the rights and interests of women, legislation had been passed to eliminate discrimination, and barriers to equality had been broken.

In 1972, the Equal Rights Amendment (ERA), which had been first introduced in 1923, was passed by the United States Congress. It reads: "Equality of rights under the law shall not be denied or abridged by the United States or by any state on account of sex." Thirty-eight states needed to ratify the ERA within the next 10 years for it to become part of the U.S. Constitution. In 1982, three states short, the ERA was

Above: The head of the parade of women veterans who served in the U.S. military during the Vietnam War. They are marching to the site *(opposite)* where a statue honoring Vietnam women veterans was dedicated in 1993, the first memorial honoring women's military service in Washington, D.C.

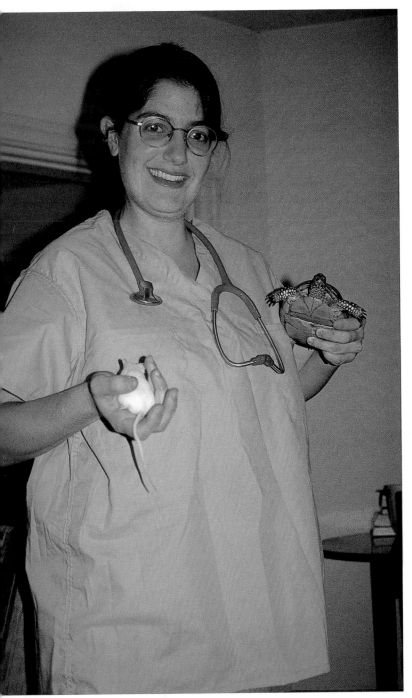

defeated. In 1993, the ERA was reintro-
duced in Congress. So, the fight to pass
the ERA continues. Women are still
fighting for equal opportunities for
women of all racial and ethnic groups
and classes, and to address issues of concern to women, such as women's health
care, reproductive rights, and safety from
violence and abuse.

Beyond the "glass ceiling"

"Glass ceiling," or the invisible obstacle
that limits workers' advancement, is a
term the U.S. Department of Labor uses
to describe "the artificial barriers, based
on attitudinal or organizational bias, that
prevent qualified individuals from
advancing within their organization and
reaching their full potential." Because
of the "glass ceiling" women are still
underrepresented in leadership
positions in high-paying and prestigious
professions such as medicine, law, and
business, despite the advances they have
made toward equality. Women are also
underrepresented in political offices and
the highest ranks of educational and
religious organizations.

Although the problem has existed for
a long time, the term "glass ceiling"
was first used in a newspaper article in
1986. The phenomenon is now widely
understood and efforts are being made
to eliminate it. The Department of
Labor recently established a Glass
Ceiling Commission to develop
strategies to help people shatter the

"glass ceiling." Books full of advice are being written. Conferences are being held to discuss strategies and educate employers about the problem. "Many of the people keeping women from moving up don't even know they are doing it. Sometimes it's subconscious, subtle discrimination," says Joyce Miller, director of the U.S. Labor Department Glass Ceiling Commission.

Certainly some women have advanced beyond the "glass ceiling." In fact, women have found that there is no "glass ceiling" in the newly-developed biotechnological industry because it lacks the longstanding traditions and practices of other businesses. At Immu-Logic Pharmaceutical Corporation, five of the company's 10 senior officers are women. "The people starting biotechnology companies are young, more open-minded, and out of a non-traditional background. There is less interest in the sex of the person than hiring them on technical and skills expertise," says Martha J. Carter, a vice-president at ImmuLogic.

As the women in the United States move toward the 21st century, they will continue to move beyond many barriers and ceilings. The composition of the family is being redefined. So is the national agenda as contemporary women demand action on issues that historically have been ignored or slighted, including access to proper health care, fair employment practices, racial equality, quality child care, and control of their bodies.

Opposite: Melinda Franceschini, a student at Tufts University Veterinary School.

Above: Arati Prabhakar, the first woman to win a Ph.D. in applied physics at the prestigious California Institute of Technology.

chapter three

Women in Society

Women's contributions to U.S. society are perhaps more significant than men's because American women have had to overcome many legal and attitudinal obstacles. Women have always had the primary responsibility for maintaining the home and family. They still do today, but with new laws that prevent discrimination against women and changing attitudes, rapidly increasing numbers of women of all ages, races, and classes are involved in every aspect of American society.

Politics

American politics has long depended on women to mail campaign literature, telephone voters, hand out material at malls and on the streets, go door-to-door, give parties, raise money, and be loyal wives, friends, and supporters. Every successful male politician has an ardent and unsung corps of female volunteers.

Increasingly, women are stepping out from behind the men. In 1992, a record number of women were elected to Congress including the first black female senator, Carol Mosley Braun. Both senators from California are women—Barbara Boxer and Diane Feinstein, a first in U.S. history. Three state governors are women: Joan Finney in Kansas, Barbara Roberts in Oregon, and Ann Richards in Texas. There are more women in state and local political office. Acknowledging the influence and power of women, President Bill Clinton appointed three women to his cabinet, including Janet Reno, the first woman attorney general.

Opposite: More and more women in the United States are working to elect candidates who support their views on women's issues.

Right: Janet Reno, first woman attorney general of the United States.

Cracking open the system "There are those who say I'm impatient, impetuous, uppity, rude, profane, brash, and overbearing. But whatever I am...I am a very serious woman," former Congresswoman Bella Abzug once said. In 1970 Abzug became the first Jewish woman ever elected to Congress where she became known as "Battling Bella" because of her outspoken involvement in the civil rights movement, the women's movement, and the peace movement. A long list of women like Abzug have dented, bruised, and finally cracked open the all-male political system that has governed the United States at all political levels. Battling the political establishment all the way, Shirley Chisholm, who grew up in poverty, was elected to the New York State Assembly in 1964 and the U.S. House of Representatives in 1968. In 1972 Chisholm announced her candidacy for the Democratic Party's nomination for president of the United States. Although she lost, one of her male opponents admitted that with a little money and organization, "she might have defeated us all." In 1987, Chisholm told a group of women state legislators, "I am Shirley Chisholm, a bearer of a double jeopardy in this nation because I am simultaneously a woman and a black person. And if I dared to do the things that I've been able to achieve in spite of my gender and my race, then every one of you in this room must dare..."

And there have been other women— Pat Schroeder, today the most senior ranking woman in Congress, was first elected to Congress in 1972. A lawyer, wife, and mother, Schroeder dealt with innuendoes about women politicians by meeting voters and saying, "Hi! I'm that nut you've been hearing about...the one who leaps over barricades uttering obscenities, the one who keeps the kids in the freezer." In 1964, Patsy Mink became the first Japanese-American woman elected to Congress, the youngest member of Congress, and the first woman elected from the new state of Hawaii. A founder of the Women's Political Caucus, Mink is an articulate critic of America's progress on social issues: "We self-righteously expect all others to admire us for our democracy and our traditions. We are so smug about our superiority, we fail to see our own glaring faults, such as prejudice and poverty amidst affluence."

Although men still hold most of the political offices in the United States, women voters and women politicians have become a force to reckon with. Men politicians can no longer ignore dealing with issues that concern women such as day care for children, divorce-law reform, health care, and a woman's right to make decisions including the right to choose to have an abortion.

Above: Every year, the U.S. Congress declares March as Women's History Month. This banner hanging above the entrance of the courthouse in Newark, New Jersey, proclaims it.

Opposite: After women won the right to vote, they established the League of Women Voters to educate and encourage women voters. An active and influential organization today, the League continues its work.

Legal

Today women receive more than 40% of law degrees. Women lawyers work for corporations, private law firms, the government, social service agencies, and public interest organizations. Two women, out of nine justices, are members of the U.S. Supreme Court, and increasing numbers of women are serving as judges in local, state, and federal courts. However, women still have a long way to go to achieve equality in the legal system.

When it was first established, the legal system in the United States was shaped by the attitude that women are inferior to men. Changing it has been a long and arduous task. In the late 1800s, women such as Elizabeth Cady Stanton and Susan B. Anthony forced state legislators to pass Married Women's Acts that separated husbands and wives under the law and allowed women to hold title to their own property, control their own wages, and be responsible for their own legal affairs.

The Equal Pay Act In 1963, Congress passed the Equal Pay Act. First introduced by Helen Gahagan Douglass, the Equal Pay Act was the first federal law which prohibited sex discrimination. Douglass was a widely acclaimed actor and singer in the 1920s. Her conscience was awakened during the Great Depression. "We ran head on into the migrants of those days, thousands of them, living in boxcars and caves dug out of the sides of the hills. ...I was shocked, and I really came of age at this time," she later explained. "I got into politics step by step."

The first woman lawyer

In 1879, Belva Lockwood was the first woman admitted to practice before the U.S. Supreme Court. Lockwood, an ardent feminist, was instrumental in advancing the national status of women. Refused admission to three Washington, D.C., law schools on the grounds that she would distract young male students, Lockwood studied law independently until she was admitted to National University Law School. She had to petition the president of the United States to get her diploma, and, later, she had to lobby the Congress to pass a law to admit her to the Supreme Court. In 1884 and 1888 she ran for president of the United States. At the age of 76, Lockwood successfully argued a case before the Supreme Court and won a huge financial award for her clients, a Cherokee Indian tribe.

In 1964, Congress passed Title VII of the Civil Rights Act, spearheaded by black civil rights lawyer Pauli Murray and lawyer and Congresswoman Martha Griffith, which, among other things, makes it illegal to fire a woman because of pregnancy or marriage.

In the 1970s, women began winning court battles against sex discrimination. In one case the Supreme Court awarded female workers retroactive pay increases

A recent study of the justice system in the state of Florida showed that women lose out financially in divorce cases, women serve more time in prison than men do for the same offenses, and female lawyers are treated as inferiors in the courtroom by many male lawyers and judges.

to give them the same salaries as men holding the same jobs. Ruth Bader Ginsburg, a lawyer and constitutional scholar, argued and won several key cases before the Supreme Court. In 1993, Ginsburg was appointed to the Supreme Court by President Bill Clinton and confirmed by the U.S. Senate, becoming the second woman on the Supreme Court. "The richness of the diversity of this country is a treasure, and it's a constant challenge, too, to remain tolerant and respectful of one another," she said at her confirmation.

Twenty-five facts about U.S. women

1. In 1990, females were 51.2% of the total U.S. population. Of this percentage, 42.9% were white females, 6.5% were black females.

2. The United States is becoming more racially diverse. According to the Census Bureau, between 1970 and 1989, the nonwhite proportion of the population increased from 12% to 16%. The fastest growing group is people of Hispanic origin, which increased from 4% in 1970 to 8% in 1989. In 1989, there were more women than men in almost every racial group.

3. U.S. females outlive males by almost seven years.

4. In 1990, the majority of adults (age 18 and over) of both sexes were currently married and living with their spouse—59% of white women; 55% of Hispanic women; 34% of black women.

5. In 1990, one out of every four children lived with one parent—usually the mother.

6. In 1990, 58% of all U.S. women were in the labor force and are projected to comprise 62% of the U.S. work force in the year 2000.

7. In 1990, 46% of all women workers were employed in relatively low-paying occupations such as secretaries, waitresses, and health aides.

8. In 1990, women represented 99% of secretaries; 84.8% of health aides, except nursing; 51.5% of bus drivers; 21.5% of farm workers; 19.3% of physicians; 18.7% of laborers, except in construction; 13.9% of police officers; 11% of military personnel on active duty; 8% of engineers; 2.6% of the top officers at the largest U.S. companies; 1.9% of jobs in the construction trades.

9. In 1991, the average earnings of women working full time were 30% less than men working full time.

10. Women represent two-thirds of all U.S. adults living in poverty.

11. Employed wives spend twice as much time on homemaking tasks as employed husbands.

12. In 1989, females earned more degrees than men at all educational levels after high school except at the highest degree level, the doctorate: 57% of all associate degrees; 53% of all bachelor's degrees; 52% of all master's degrees; 36% of all doctorates.

13. In 1989, women were awarded 41% of all law degrees, 33% of all medical degrees, and 26% of all dentistry degrees.

14. In 1990, the percentage of female college faculty in the field of physics was 3.2%; in engineering 6.6%; in law 19%; in theology 22.8%; in economics 22.8%; in computer

science 25%; in business, commerce, and marketing 35.5%; in art, drama, and music 37.8%; in education 45.7%; in foreign languages 59.6%; and in home economics 99.9%.

15. In 1992, women comprised 20.4% of state legislators in the 50 states with 4.3% in the state of Kentucky, 16.1% in New York, 23.3% in California, 23.7% in Hawaii, and 39.5% in Washington.

16. In the 1992 election, the percentage of women doubled from 5% to 10% in the U.S. Congress—48 women serve in the House of Representatives and six women serve in the U.S. Senate. Of the 54 women, 14 are women of color.

17. In 1990, women comprised 13% of all federal judges.

18. In 1991, 17% of all elected mayors were female, up from 1% in 1971.

19. In the United States, more than 1.13 million incidents of domestic violence against women are reported to police yearly.

20. In 1992, a U.S. woman was killed by her husband or boyfriend every 14 days.

21. An estimated two to three million women in the U.S. are lesbians.

22. In 42 states, lesbians can be fired from their jobs because of their sexual orientation.

23. Of all practicing artists, 40% are women, yet only 3% of the artworks in public collections in museums in the United States are by women.

24. In 1992, a survey found an increase from 15% in 1982 to 24% in 1992 in the number of never-married women, aged 18 to 44, who have children. A significant proportion are older, well-educated, financially-secure women.

    According to a researcher, these women are choosing "to have a baby without the hassle of marriage."

25. In a national survey, 75% to 95% of U.S. women credit the feminist campaign with improving their lives. An overwhelming majority of women think that the women's movement should continue working for improvements.

Business and finance

In 1992, just 3% of top executives in large corporations were women; but, with women holding 40% of the entry-level and middle management jobs, double their share in 1972, there are a lot of women in business on their way up. U.S. businesses are scrambling to accommodate women workers, especially in light of some well-known court cases against large corporations over sex discrimination in hiring and promotion. Some corporations provide child care facilities. Many run seminars to deal with issues such as sexual harassment.

Sue Lutz May is one of the first women to have made a career in the financial management aspect of banking.

One success story Jane Hirsh is a businesswoman who has been around. In 1972, when she was 30 years old, Hirsh borrowed $300 from a friend and started Copley Pharmaceutical, Inc., a company that reproduces brand-name drugs when their patent protection expires. Twenty-one years later Hoechst Celanese Corporation agreed to buy 51% of Copley stock for $546 million in cash, about $148 million of which will go to Hirsh. She will also retain 13% of the company's stock and stay on as chief executive and chairperson of the board of directors. "We were blown away by Jane Hirsh," said Bruce Bennett, the general manager for Hoechst. "She has a grasp of everything that's going on in a complex operation…" According to Hirsh, "I care about people, product development, equipment, and manufacturing. It isn't sexy but it sure is practical and profitable."

Hirsh works long hours to run her business and care for her three children. But she doesn't complain. "I'm too upbeat to do something that isn't fun," she says.

Bleak outlook Most women, however, work in the other end of business—in clerical positions and support staff. They also make up two-thirds of the growing contingent work force—part-time and temporary workers—who do not have any job security, health insurance, or other benefits. A recent study showed that women of color work harder for less money because they are concentrated in occupations that pay low wages. Karen Nussbaum is determined to improve employment opportunities for women workers. A former clerical worker herself and union organizer, Nussbaum was recently appointed head of the Women's Bureau of the U.S. Labor Department. Prior to her appointment, Nussbaum was head of 9 to 5, the national Association of Working Women.

Even though more and more women are joining the work force, most of them are confined to low-paying clerical positions.

The majority of teachers in U.S. schools may be women, but few women occupy top management posts in education.

Education

Since the 1970s, legal barriers to women's educational opportunities have been removed. In addition, cultural attitudes have shifted away from viewing the education of females as either harmful or wasteful. Today women earn the majority of degrees at all educational levels except doctorates. Nevertheless, women have a long way to go—they are grossly under-represented in traditionally male strongholds such as engineering and physical sciences. They are rarely found in upper management positions such as heads of school districts or colleges. And recent studies show that girls still face discrimination in the classroom from teachers and male classmates and in the way material is presented in textbooks and tests. Broad-based national organizations such as the American Association of University Women are working hard to promote education and equity for girls and women in the United States.

An extraordinary list of dedicated

Mary McLeod Bethune

Born into a slave family, Mary McLeod Bethune (1875–1955) was the most influential African-American woman in the United States for over 30 years. An educator and civil rights activist, Bethune (seen here addressing the American Soviet Friendship Rally in November 1944) founded the Daytona Normal and Industrial School for Negro Girls, now the Bethune-Cookman College in Daytona Beach, Florida. A 17-foot statue erected in 1974 shows Bethune with an African-American girl and boy. Her words are carved around the base of the statue: "I leave you love, I leave you hope. I leave you the challenge of developing confidence in one another. I leave you respect for the use of power. I leave you faith. I leave you racial dignity."

Equal rights in education

The American Association of University Women (AAUW) represents 135,000 college graduates and is the nation's leading advocate of educational equality for women and girls. Its current executive director is Anne L. Bryant, an administrator and educator. She testifies before Congress, advocating equity for women and girls in education, the workplace, and the family. She also participates in AAUW state and regional meetings, and serves as a spokesperson for the AAUW to organizations and media throughout the United States. As director of the AAUW, Bryant serves on the boards of various national and international organizations. She also publishes numerous articles in professional publications.

women have led the drive to prove that women were as bright as men, and as deserving of a good education. In the 19th century, Catherine Beecher was a very successful crusader in training women as teachers. Beecher was born into a family that believed girls should be educated. She passed on her good fortune by opening teacher training schools, including the Western Female Institute that trained teachers for the sparsely settled regions of the western United States. Through her efforts, more than 30,000 female teachers were trained for western schools.

Education for blacks Mary McLeod Bethune devoted her life to improving educational opportunities for black children. She was educated in mission schools and wanted to become a missionary. However, she was rejected twice and, instead, became a teacher. In 1904, she opened a school for the children of black families who worked for rich white people, today's Bethune-Cookman College. One of the most influential black leaders of her day, Bethune received many honors and served in a number of important positions.

Entertainment

More women are being hired as television reporters and movie directors. "Five years ago there were three women directors," Nora Ephron said in 1991. "Now there are over 20. It's not enough, but it's a gigantic change." Women entertainers are also venturing into business: television host Oprah Winfrey has her own production company, and Madonna has made herself into a multi-million dollar business. So has Dolly Parton, a composer, singer, actor, and entrepreneur who has won every country singing and song-writing award there is to win several times. Committed to helping people achieve economic self-sufficiency, Parton built "Dollywood," a theme park in eastern Tennessee, and is the major employer in the area.

Many female entertainers have become politically active. Barbra Streisand, a singer and film actor, producer, and director, is active in a number of causes. Born in 1942, Streisand got her start by winning a talent contest in 1961. In 1968, she won an Academy Award, the highest award in the movie industry, for her performance in *Funny Girl*. In 1991, there was a furor when the Academy of Motion Pictures did not nominate *Prince of Tides*, a movie Streisand directed and starred in, for any major awards. Many people felt that *Prince of Tides*, despite being very successful, was ignored because Streisand is an independent and powerful woman.

Dolly Parton is known all over the world as an outstanding entertainer.

Although women are making important inroads in the entertainment industry, many movies and television programs still depict women as airheads, or as objects to be pursued or purchased, beaten up, raped, killed, or rescued and taken care of by a man.

Pearl Buck was the first American woman to win the Nobel Prize for Literature.

Art and literature

Women are moving into top management positions in art institutions and museums. One such achiever is Agnes Gund, president of the Metropolitan Museum of Art in New York City. In 1990 Jenny Holzer was chosen to represent the United States in the prestigious Venice Biennale, the first time a woman's work was chosen to exclusively represent the United States. Holzer won the Biennale's grand prize.

According to the American Association of Museums, 40% of all practicing artists today are women. However, their work is not yet represented in American museums since only 3% of the artwork in museums is by women. To help remedy this situation, the National Museum of Women in the Arts in Washington, D.C., was founded in 1987 to record, preserve, display, and support art by women.

Women writers Although male writers still dominate literature and the theater in the United States, women are on the move. In 1993, Toni Morrison won the Nobel Prize for Literature, the first African-American woman and second American woman to win the internationally prestigious honor. More women are becoming top literary agents, book and magazine publishers, and authors. More creative outlets are being created for women: *Sojourner: The Women's Forum*, a feminist newspaper committed to publishing writings by and for women; KITCHEN TABLE: Women of Color Press, a publishing company that only publishes and distributes the writing of Third World women of all racial/cultural heritages and sexual orientations; and Lesbian Herstory Archives, an archive that collects writings by lesbians and material about lesbian oppression and liberation.

Throughout American history, there have always been women writers. During the colonial period, Phillis Wheatley came to America as a slave and was bought by the Wheatley family. She had a quick mind and a great capacity for learning, and Mrs. Wheatley decided to educate her. Phillis studied many subjects, including Latin, Greek, mathematics, and history. At the age of 13, she began writing poetry. Before long, white intellectuals began to admire her. She gained her freedom, but died at the age of 31. Her only book, *Poems on Various Subjects, Religious and Moral*, was published in England in 1773.

Louisa May Alcott wrote during the 19th century. Considered a writer of novels for juveniles, Alcott achieved world fame for her best-selling book, *Little Women*, which is still widely read. As did other well-educated women of her time, Alcott supported her family with her writing.

In the early 20th century, Pearl Buck became the first American woman to win the Nobel Prize for Literature. Buck's parents were missionaries and she grew up in China and learned to speak Chinese before English. According to Buck, she became "mentally bifocal." Buck was a prolific writer and many of her books centered on regional and universal elements of Chinese life.

Music and dance

A new generation of women is determined to change things in music and dance. Despite being told that girls can't be conductors, Marin Alsop became one anyhow. Today she conducts the Eugene, Oregon, symphony orchestra. "Things can only get brighter for conductors who are also women," Alsop says. The same is also true for women composers and musicians.

The well-reviewed and popular Women's Philharmonic, based in San Francisco, California, is known as the voice for women composers, conductors, and musicians. In the final concert of the 1992-1993 season, pianist Emily Hsieh, a 15-year-old prodigy, played Amy Beach's *Piano Concerto*. Beach, who

Little Women brought fame to Louisa May Alcott.

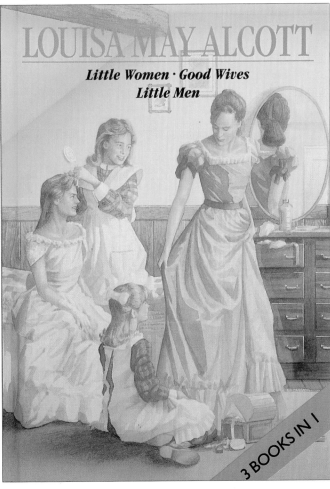

concerto, a string quartet, a one-act opera, and a great many songs.

Women artists are becoming more visible and popular in rap and rock—Queen Latifah, MC Lyte, Melissa Etheridge, L7, Babes in Toyland, Tracy Chapman, and the riot grrrls. In country music, women performers such as Mary-Chapin Carpenter and Lorrie Morgan are writing lyrics and singing songs that question the traditional stand-by-your-man-no-matter-what-he-does philosophy of traditional country music.

At age 81, Katherine Dunham is still devoting her time and energy to dance. A pioneer in bringing black culture to the American stage, Dunham started out studying anthropology. After spending two years studying tribal dances in the West Indies, Dunham dropped anthro-

JoAnn Falletta has been called "one of the most promising conductors of her generation."

died in 1944, was the first person in America to write a symphony of importance. Although she had only a single year of study of harmony, Beach composed 150 opuses, including a piano

"Every major orchestra and opera company in the United States owes its continued existence largely to the dedicated support of women, and most can trace their origins to the vision and determination of one woman. But these institutions still give women practically no attention as composers or conductors, though most now have women players."
—*music critic Joseph McLellan*

pology and focused on performing dances of both urban and tribal black people. In 1939, she started the first of several companies—the Tropical Revue, Katherine Dunham Dance Company, and later the Katherine Dunham School of Cultural Arts. With her dance company, Dunham toured the United States during the time when segregation was common. "I shall not appear here again until people like me can sit with people like you," she once told an audience that had just given her a standing ovation.

"It takes great passion and great energy to do anything creative, especially in the theater. You have to care so much that you can't sleep, you can't eat, you can't talk to people. It's just got to be right. You can't do it without that passion."
—*Agnes De Mille, dancer and choreographer*

Saxophonist Kit McClure and her All Woman Band performing at an outdoor concert.

Science and technology

In 1972, Sandra Kurtzig founded a computer company. In 1976 Chien-Shiung Wu, a nuclear physicist, received the National Medal of Science, the highest science award in the United States. In 1983, Barbara McClintock won the Nobel Prize for her genetic research. That same year, Dr. Sally K. Ride became the first American woman

astronaut to make a space flight. Slowly, but surely, women continue to move into a wide variety of careers in science and technology.

According to Wu, a Chinese-born physicist, "The traditional roles of wife and mother and the role of dedicated scientist are actually compatible. Isn't it more satisfying for a woman to have her own intellectual endeavor along with the responsibility of home and children?" In 1936, Wu immigrated to the United States. Four years later, she received a Ph.D. from the University of California at Berkeley. She became a professor at Smith College, sharing her knowledge and her love for science with students who were not much younger than she was.

When the United States entered World War II, she volunteered to join other brilliant scientists in finding ways for science to help America win the war. In 1954, Wu became an American citizen.

A member of the faculty at Columbia University in New York City, Wu is known as one of the world's leading experimental physicists. In particular she is famous for her experiment that disproved the "law of parity" which stated that like nuclear particles always acted alike. In 1956 physicists Tsung-dao Lee and Chen Ning Yang theorized that the "law of parity" does not hold for weak interactions of subatomic particles. Wu designed and performed the experiment that proved Lee's and Yang's theory. Although Lee and Yang won the Nobel Prize for Physics, Wu was overlooked. However she has won many honors and awards and is considered a strong candidate for a Nobel Prize.

Today, Wu continues her research at Columbia University.

Health care

Today women make up 26.6% of physicians. In addition the majority of other health-care workers such as nurses and lab technicians are women. Recent studies have documented the male bias in medical research and treatment. Until two years ago, the National Institute of Health allocated only 13% of its budget to women's health. Today the idea of "women's medicine" is being discussed seriously and women's centers are springing up across the United States.

In 1919, Harvard Medical School hired Alice Hamilton to teach industrial medicine, and she became the first woman on the faculty. Harvard did not want to hire a woman, but they had no choice. Hamilton was the first person to study industrial diseases and industrial hygiene in the United States and there was no man who knew as much as she did. Born in 1869, Hamilton devoted her career as a doctor to the health of working people. She spent years identifying health hazards in mines and factories. She pioneered the field of industrial medicine and pushed state and federal governments to force employers to provide safeguards for working people. Hamilton not only examined patients, but also climbed into mines and conducted on-site investigations of factories. Long before concerns about air and water pollution became popular, she had documented the hazards and raised the issues.

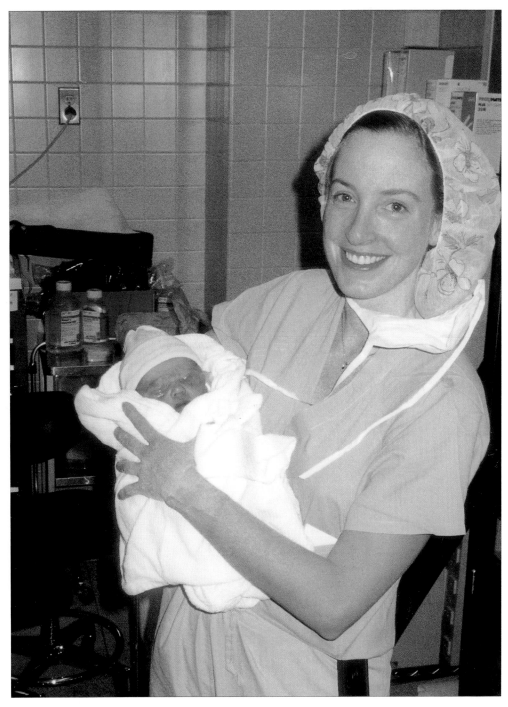

Opposite: First Lady Hillary Rodham Clinton is seen here discussing health care reform and women's health issues at Holy Name Hospital in Teaneck, New Jersey, the site of Women's Health Source, northern New Jersey's first hospital-based women's health center.

Left: Dr. Nancy Ripp with a newborn baby.

Super coach

C. Vivian Stringer is the basketball coach of the top-ranked University of Iowa women's basketball team. In 1992, she was named National Coach of the Year, an honor she also received in 1988. Stringer and her women's basketball! teams have compiled an amazing list of records.

According to Stringer, being a coach is very demanding, but it's worth it because she is teaching young women how to handle themselves on the basketball court as well as off the court. "I get a tremendous amount of pleasure from working with young women. It's gratifying to help them understand that they can be the best in whatever it is that they choose to do."

Sports

Almost 69% of American women participate in sports or fitness activities. Since Congress passed a law in 1972 forbidding sex discrimination in schools that get money from the federal government, the number of girls and colleges participating in sports has soared. Professional women's sports is a multimillion dollar business. Women athletes continue to set new records.

Hard hats

Although their numbers are still small, women are driving bulldozers, climbing telephone poles, building houses, and doing other traditionally male jobs that pay high wages.

Frieda Maldonado, a single mother of four, learned how to operate a front-end loader at an organization called Nontraditional Employment for Women (NEW). "I still remember when we went there and decided I'd go into construction, my kids said I was crazy. Now they think I'm great and my youngest daughter is going to take the test for the union. Maybe we'll make it a mother-daughter union," she said.

Started 14 years ago, NEW trains women to be carpenters, plumbers, electricians, heavy machine operators, and construction workers. Such jobs are called blue-collar jobs, but they pay considerably higher wages than the so-called pink-collar jobs women traditionally do, such as secretaries and

clerical workers. Women have had a tough time breaking down the male-guarded barriers to blue-collar jobs. But programs like NEW make it easier.

During the 13-week program, women learn skills and lift weights to build up their strength. Gardenia White, the executive director, works closely with employers to help women get jobs. Today more than 1,300 women hard hats in New York City were trained at NEW. That's only a fraction of a percent of all construction workers, but it's a start.

In 1993, Anne Marie Mahoney graduated from Nontraditional Employment for Women. In this picture, she is studying an instrument panel at a huge utilities company. Today she drives a railroad train.

Uniforms

In 1990, Elizabeth M. Watson became the first woman to head the police force of any of the 20 largest cities in the United States. There are women police officers and fire fighters in towns and cities throughout the United States. Women are also playing a significant role in the U.S. military.

In 1993, Mary F. Rabadeau, a former Catholic school teacher, became the chief of police in Elizabeth, New Jersey, a working-class city of 110,000 residents. A 14-year veteran of the police force, Captain Rabadeau was one of the first five women to join the department. She decided to become a police officer after listening to a speech about police work

Amelia Earhart

Amelia Earhart, a pioneer aviator, achieved many records, including being the first woman pilot to fly across the Atlantic Ocean and the first person ever to make a solo flight from Hawaii to the U.S. mainland. She disappeared over the Pacific Ocean during an attempted around-the-world flight in 1937. Today there are several memorials to Earhart all over the United States. In her own words, "Women must try to do things as men have tried. When they fail, failure must be but a challenge to others."

at the Catholic elementary school where she had taught for eight years. As director of the Elizabeth Police Department, Rabadeau is the first woman to lead a major police department in New Jersey and one of the few women heading police departments in the country.

Activists and volunteers

Throughout U.S. history, charitable organizations, religious groups, and reform movements were mainly made up of women. Today women volunteer at homeless shelters, fight for environmental causes, work for peace, and serve without pay in a variety of ways to improve society.

Above: Kim Heveron is a ranger with the U.S. National Park Service.

Left: Women workers on strike.

Opposite: A member of the New York City Park police.

Being Woman

omen have progressed quite far in the United States. They have unprecedented opportunities and freedom. Nevertheless, women still have far to go, especially women of color and poor women. Violence against women is rampant in U.S. homes and streets. Close to half of all employed women work in relatively low-paying jobs such as health aides and secretaries. For every dollar earned by American men, American women earn 72 cents. Women with both careers and families carry the bulk of domestic and child care responsibilities. Women are vastly underrepresented in the judicial and political systems.

Opposite: Chris McGoey is a feminist lawyer and activist.

Right: Liz Roslewicz *(left)* and Jackie Magness *(right)*, co-founders of Light Works, Inc., a non-profit educational organization dedicated to changing lives through moments of insight. Their T-shirts show the U.S. Capitol Building printed on the bottom and many parachutes carrying the symbol for women above it. The message reads: "We're coming in!'

Women's issues

Being a woman in the United States is a challenge. Countless experts, frequently men, offer opinions on male/female relations, commonly called the "war between the sexes." Issues that are defined as women's issues such as date rape, sexual assault, incest, child care, abortion, and menopause are discussed and debated, often by men with women as the audience, in countless books, articles, and television and radio programs. Women are bombarded with propaganda from all directions—advertisers, religious leaders, mental health professionals—about how they should act, look, and think.

Laura J. Waterman is a single mother by choice. According to Laura, her "wonderful son" Joshua has a multi-generational network of loving and caring honorary mothers, aunts, and grandmothers.

Women on the move Despite all this, being a woman in the United States is also very exciting. Throughout society, women are on the move. They are joining together in small and large numbers to fight for justice and equality. They are transcending traditions and stereotypes and creating new ways of being a woman in the United States.

Redefining the family

According to the U.S. Census Bureau, the two largest family groups in the United States are "married couples without children at home" and "married couples with at least one child under 18 living at home." Since 1970, the percentage of "married couples without children at home" has remained fairly constant at about 30% of the population. However, "married couples with at least one child under 18 living at home" has shrunk from 40% of all U.S. households in 1970 to 26% in 1991. The number of single-parent families with children has increased drastically from 3.8 million, or 12.9%, in 1970 to 10.1 million, or 29%, in 1991. Women head almost 90% of these single-parent families.

Only 10% of the families in the United States today fit the traditional middle- and upper-middle-class image of a husband who earns the living with a wife who stays home to raise their children. In fact, U.S. families are diverse and include families comprised of stepparents and stepchildren, single-parent families, lesbian and gay families, families with a stay-at-home father, and high-paid, fast-paced, two-career couples. Families are interracial and interreligious.

Women have been and continue to be the emotional and psychological glue in most U.S. families. They carry out the celebrations for birthdays, anniversaries, and holidays; tend to hurt feelings and disappointments; nurture children and take care of elderly relatives. Women also do the bulk of cooking, cleaning, shopping, and other household tasks.

Various cultural and religious traditions play a strong part in determining a woman's role in society. Some religious groups, such as Roman Catholicism and Orthodox Judaism, impose absolute prohibitions against the use of birth control. Other religious groups have taken a militant stand against abortion. Cultural groups such as Hispanics have longstanding traditional role expectations for women that include being deferential to men and taking care of their families. Women from traditional Asian-American families are expected to confine their activities to the home. According to Margaret Chin, an Asian-American woman who ran for political office, her mother initially opposed her political aspirations because "a daughter doesn't go out and mind other people's business."

New role models Contemporary women in the United States from all cultural, ethnic, and religious groups are questioning and redefining traditional roles and models. Margaret Chin seeks

The two-parent family is no longer the norm in the United States.

People in the United States are beginning to speak out against violence toward women, which many experts call an epidemic. The owner of this car has placed a sticker protesting violence against women on the car's back bumper.

a political office because "I want a seat at the table (where decisions are made) and (want to) open the door for others." Hung Liu, an Asian-American artist, uses her art to challenge the stereotype of Asian women as exotic concubines. Maria Blanco is a co-founder of Latinas for Reproductive Choice, an organization dedicated to dispelling the myth that Latinas don't have abortions and aren't pro-choice. "Abortion isn't only a white issue. We are having abortions at a rate that is 60% higher than non-Latinas." Blanco is also concerned about disseminating information to Latinas about contraceptives and prenatal care. Abby Abinati, the first Native American to practice law in California, is the legal director of the National Center for Lesbian Rights (NCLR). The Lesbian of Color Project was started by the NCLR to work on such issues as "immigration for women whose sexual orientation forced them to leave their own countries."

Dealing with poverty

In 1989, about 18% of children in the United States lived in families with incomes below the federal poverty line. Most of those children lived in households headed by women and included 39.8% of all black children, 38.8% of Native American children, 32.2% of Hispanic children, 17.1% of Asian-American children, and 12.5% of white children.

Women also constitute 71% of elderly poor people. A recent study of women over age 40 who got divorced, found that more than half of them had difficulty keeping up payments on their homes, making repairs, and paying utility bills. Nearly two out of three of the divorced women lost the family home. The number of divorced fathers who fail to provide court-ordered financial support for their children is a national epidemic. Poverty in the United States is clearly female.

Why are women poor? There are four primary reasons for women's poverty: first, lack of access to high paying jobs; second, the result of doing "women's work" either in the low-paying jobs with few, if any, benefits or in the non-paying job with no financial benefits of raising children and keeping house; third, laws and practices that have until recently limited women's ability to secure business loans, obtain credit, and claim their share of marital assets; and fourth, women's lack of confidence and experience because of the longstanding stereotype that women can't handle money.

Increasingly, women in the United States are taking responsibility for their financial well-being. Poor women are organizing self-help groups. They are lobbying politicians to provide education and job training. The D.C. Citywide Welfare Rights Organization, Inc., in Washington, D.C., provides assistance and workshops for welfare recipients to

Poverty in the United States is predominantly female.

Some women have been very successful in their careers. Tina Brown is the editor of the *New Yorker*, a magazine with a wide appeal.

"Despite the gains of the last quarter century, many women still cling to the belief that handling money is a man's job, derived from intrinsic knowledge that women simply do not possess. As a result, women resist taking responsibility for their financial well-being."

—*Jane Bryant Quinn, financial*

help them understand their rights. A group called Poor/Working-Class Lesbians gives financial aid to lesbians with emergency survival needs. The Divorce Hotline in Illinois provides a 24-hour telephone service with information about emergency shelter and other services. Divorce Equity in Ohio offers research, advocacy, and education in the divorce process. More and more books about women and money are available including *A Woman's Book of Money: A Guide to Financial Independence* by Sylvia Auerbach and *The Joy of Money: The Guide to Women's Financial Freedom* by Paula Nelson.

Dealing with violence

Violence is everywhere in the United States. It's in the movies—one out of eight Hollywood movies depicts a rape theme. It's on television—by age 18 the average youth has watched 250,000 acts of violence and 40,000 attempted murders. It's in American homes—31% of all female homicide victims in 1988 were killed by their husbands or boyfriends, and three to four million American women a year are beaten by their husbands, ex-husbands, or boyfriends. It's outside the home—one woman in four will be sexually assaulted in her lifetime. According to a study by the National Victim Center, 73% of women limit the places they will go alone due to fear of attack versus 45% of men.

Self-preservation In a variety of ways, women are striving to protect themselves, including learning self-defense, establishing a network of battered-women's shelters and telephone hotlines, lobbying for legislation, and protesting the way women are portrayed in advertising and the media. As of 1989, all states have laws against domestic violence. On the national level, the U.S Center for Disease Control and Prevention is launching a program aimed at curbing the growing epidemic of violence against women. At the local level, there are many organizations including Seattle Rape Relief (SRR). Founded in 1972, one of the first rape crisis centers in the United States, SRR offers services to survivors of sexual assault, community advocacy programs, and youth education. Women Against Violence Everywhere (WAVE) is a newly formed citywide coalition in New York City.

Students at a protest meeting against rape.

"The name is so encompassing because we are against violence everywhere," says Martha Bright, a founder of WAVE. "Violence is in our schools, homes, churches, and streets, and it's also hidden." According to Gwen Braxton, another founder of WAVE and program director of the national Black Women's Health Project, Medgar Evers College, "Poverty is violence; having to choose between sterilization and abortion is violence; having a child taken away is violence; verbal abuse is violence; sexual harassment is violence; police harassment is violence; even the ugliness of our city and what is being done to our physical environment is violence. The limited choice open to black children is violence—they can sell drugs, become prostitutes, or go to war—this too is violence."

Native American women, who live scattered throughout the United States on 287 reservations, are mobilizing to stop domestic violence in Native American families. According to a spouse-abuse prevention manual written by a Native American for Native

Right: As crimes against women get wider publicity, more and more women are now taking self-defense classes.

Opposite: In 1990, Representative Louisa Slaughter introduced legislation that would make October National Domestic Violence Awareness Month.

Americans, domestic abuse is not a Native American tradition. Some activists say that it is the result of alcohol and Christianity that was introduced by Europeans into Native American culture hundreds of years ago. It has become worse in modern times due to extremely high unemployment and geographic isolation on the reservations. The women's groups include the American Indian Women's Circle Against Abuse. "Our children need to know that at one time, a man could become chief only if the women in the tribe agreed that he should be chief," says Barbara Anders, a Sisseton-Wahpeton Dakota and chair of the Circle.

Making choices

The U.S. society is full of choices for women. Choices about how to juggle a career and family. Choices about what to think about such issues as abortion. Choices about what role to play in society. Choices about how to deal with racism and sexism. It is tough being a woman in the United States. Although women sometimes get overwhelmed and confused by the choices, they are determined to move forward and make the most of their opportunities. And, across the country countless women are working hard to overcome the problems and barriers and make it not so tough to be a woman in the United States, particularly a poor woman or a woman of color.

chapter five

Profiles of Women

T he aspirations, talents, and skills of countless women in the United States have been, and, to some extent still are, thwarted by legal and attitudinal barriers left by centuries of discrimination. Nevertheless, innumerable women have overcome the barriers and become significant and important leaders in every field: the arts, science and mathematics, technology, sports, politics, education, the humanities, industry and commerce, religion, social work, and medicine. The six women profiled in this chapter exemplify the courage, creativity, resilience, and determination that characterize women in the United States— and everywhere.

Dorothea Lynde Dix (1802–1887)

When Dorothea Lynde Dix, social reformer and crusader for the humane and scientific treatment of prisoners and mental patients, died in 1887, people around the world honored her. Her achievements were well-known all over the world and prisoners and mental patients in various countries had benefited from her efforts. Proclamations, testimonials, and tributes were spoken and printed from the United States to Japan to England. A prominent American doctor wrote: "Thus has died and been laid to rest in the most quiet unostentatious way the most useful and distinguished woman America has yet produced." In 1983, almost 100 years after her death, a U.S. postal stamp was issued in honor of Dix.

Opposite: Dorothea Lynde Dix was one of the first persons in the United States to demand more humane conditions in the treatment of mental patients and prisoners.

Right: Today more women are becoming doctors, especially in obstetrics and gynecology.

Above: Caring for the sick and mentally ill people became a lifetime crusade for Dorothea Dix.

Right: During the Civil War, Dorothea Dix served as Superintendent of Women Nurses of the Union Army. Despite demanding administrative duties, she regularly visited convalescing soldiers.

nobler purpose for which to labor, something which would fill the vacuum which I felt in my soul."

"Lunatics don't feel the cold" Dix finally found her purpose on a cold, blustery day in March 1841, 10 days before her 39th birthday. Responding to a request to teach Sunday School to women prisoners in the East Cambridge, Massachusetts, jail, Dix heard tormented moans and screams. Insisting on being shown the source of the anguish, Dix discovered two indigent mentally ill women confined in small cages made of rough boards—

A difficult childhood Dix was born in 1802. Her father was an itinerant preacher and her mother was a semi-invalid. At a young age, Dix shouldered the responsibility of caring for her mother and her two younger brothers. "I never knew a childhood" is all Dix ever said about her growing up years.

Although she became a successful teacher and writer, Dix suffered from periodic physical and mental breakdowns that left her unable to continue her normal activities. For years, she struggled to regain her enthusiasm and energy for life. In a letter to a friend, Dix wrote that she longed for "some

> **"GENTLEMEN:...I tell what I have seen. ...The condition of human beings, reduced to the most extreme states of degradation and misery, cannot be exhibited in softened language...insane persons confined within this Commonwealth in cages, closets, cellars, stalls, pens! Chained, naked, beaten with rods and lashed into obedience."**
> —*Dorothea Lynde Dix in her Memorial*

disheveled, shivering people whose only crime was their illness. No stove heated their bare, filthy pens. "Why is there no heat?" Dix asked the jailer. "Because lunatics don't feel the cold," he replied. Appalled at the conditions and the jailer's attitude (a common belief at the time), Dix went to court and succeeded in getting stoves installed.

Her consciousness raised, Dix wondered how mentally ill people were treated elsewhere. At a time when women rarely traveled, and certainly not alone, Dix went by wagon and stagecoach to every jail, almshouse, and private home in Massachusetts where indigent mentally ill people were kept. Never before in American history had any person undertaken such an extensive, systematic, and controversial investigation of a social condition. In January 1843, Dix's findings were presented in the form of a Memorial to the Massachusetts Legislature. In it she appealed in very strong terms for more humane conditions for the insane.

The reaction to Dix's Memorial was fierce. Newspaper editors blasted her in articles and editorials. Dix was stunned but resolute. Her friends rallied to support her. Prominent people checked out her findings and discovered that she was right. Slowly public opinion shifted. Finally, by a large majority, the legislature appropriated money to provide proper facilities for the care of mentally ill people.

Taking her crusade abroad For 40 years, Dix continued her crusade throughout the United States and parts of Canada. In 1854, she traveled to Scotland, the Channel Islands, Italy, Greece, Turkey, Germany, Russia, and the Scandinavian countries. Her crusade even spread to Japan through Arinori Mori, a Japanese diplomat, whom Dix had influenced when he was stationed in Washington, D.C. Several years after

On September 23, 1989, the U.S. Postal Service issued a first-day cover in honor of Dorothea Dix.

his return to Japan, Mori wrote in a letter to Dix: "My Dear Miss Dix.-During the long silence, do not think I have been idle about the matter in which you take so deep an interest. I have given the subject much of my time and attention, and have successfully established an asylum for the insane at Kyoto, and another in this city is being built and will soon be ready for its work of good. Other asylums will follow, too, and I ardently hope they will be the means of alleviating much misery."

Striking looking with clear skin, blue-gray eyes with pupils so large that sometimes her eyes looked black, and a voice described as "sweet, rich, low, perfect in enunciation and every tone pervaded with blended love and power," Dix revolutionized public attitudes and government policy toward people with mental illness. "It is time that people should have learned that to be insane is not to be disgraced; that sickness is not to be ranked with crime," she once wrote.

Dix also fought hard for vocational training for people with mental retardation, the rehabilitation of prisoners, and special training for nurses. During the Civil War, she served as the first Superintendent of Women Nurses for the Union Army.

On July 17, 1887, Dix died. According to her wishes, she was buried at Mt. Auburn Cemetery in Cambridge, Massachusetts. A simple piece of marble marks her grave. There is no epitaph or date, only her name.

Mary Harris "Mother" Jones (1830?–1930)

Mary Harris Jones called herself a "hell-raiser." And that, she was; for 50 years, Jones fought for the rights of working people—miners, railroad workers, and mill and factory workers. "No matter what your fight, don't be ladylike," Jones said.

Jones was especially fierce when employers hired children to work in mines, mills, and factories, a common

Mother Jones

practice then. During one protest meeting, Jones brought some children with her to show the crowd the effects of child labor, "I put the little boys with their fingers off and hands crushed and maimed on a platform. I held up their mutilated hands and showed them to the crowd and made the statement that Philadelphia's (Pennsylvania) mansions were built on the broken bones, the quivering hearts, and drooping heads of these little children," she wrote in her autobiography.

Tragedy strikes Born in County Cork, Ireland, Jones came with her family to Canada in the late 1830s when she was about 7 years old. She grew up to become a teacher. After a few years, she went to work as a dressmaker. In 1861, she married George Jones, an iron molder and active member of the Iron Molders Union. The couple had four children. But then, Jones's life changed forever. She described what happened in her autobiography: "In 1867 a yellow fever epidemic swept Memphis (Tennessee). Its victims were mainly among the poor and the workers. The rich and well-to-do fled the city. The dead surrounded us. ...One by one, my four little children sickened and died. I

Women factory workers assembling dolls. They worked long hours and were paid a mere pittance. Furthermore, they had no job security and the working environment was frequently hazardous to their health.

washed their little bodies and got them ready for burial. My husband caught the fever and died. I sat alone through nights of grief. No one came to me. No one could. Other homes were as stricken as was mine."

Finding her true calling After the death of her family, Jones moved to Chicago and started working again as a dressmaker. In 1871, tragedy struck her again when a fire swept through Chicago. Except for her life and the clothes she was wearing, Mary Harris Jones lost everything in the fire. She found refuge in a building where the

Noble Order of the Knights of Labor met, a nationwide labor organization that helped workers improve their lives. Jones identified immediately with the workers. "I belong to a class who has been robbed, exploited, and plundered down through the many long centuries, and because I belong to that class I have the instinct to go and break the chains," she once wrote.

The early industrial workers in the United States lived miserable lives. They usually worked 11 to 12 hours a day, six days a week for very low wages. They were not entitled to any vacations. The working conditions were

Even at the age of 98, "Mother" Jones was still an active labor leader.

unhygienic and dangerous: poor lighting, little ventilation, minimal sanitation, and no safety devices. Employers usually owned the stores where the workers shopped and the shacks where they lived. The workers were charged high prices and rent, which the owner deducted from their paychecks. At the end of the week or month, the workers got very little in terms of money. In an effort to protect themselves, more and more workers joined unions. One of the tactics they used to pressure employers was going on strike. They stopped work to protest poor working conditions or to force the employer to accept their demands for fairer treatment.

Industrial action In 1877, Jones was involved in her first strike. Then another strike and another. "My address is like my shoes; it travels with me. I abide where there is a fight against wrong," Jones wrote. She organized and encouraged workers. She raised money. When there was violence, which was all too common, she cared for the injured and buried the dead. One writer who saw Mother Jones in action wrote: "With one speech she often threw a whole community on strike and she could keep the strikers loyal month after month on

empty stomachs and behind prison bars."

Jones was repeatedly arrested and thrown in jail for holding meetings and leading protest marches or for trespassing on employers' property, or for disobeying a court order that forbid such activities. "Goodbye, boys. I'm under arrest. Keep up the fight! Don't surrender," she shouted to a group of striking miners as the police took her away. Her "boys," the men who worked in the mines, called her "Mother." So did everyone else, including newspaper reporters.

In 1903, Mother Jones went to Pennsylvania and led a group of mill children and adult workers through three states on a 20-day, 120-mile protest march against child labor. Two years after her march, the Pennsylvania Legislature passed a law regulating child labor. Other states followed suit. Finally, a federal child labor law was passed.

Even as a very old woman, Mother Jones continued raising hell. In her 80s, she was participating in New York City's streetcar and garment workers strikes. In her 90s, she was still organizing in West Virginia coal mines. Shortly after her 100th birthday, Mary Harris "Mother" Jones died. A grand monument with a tall shaft flanked by two statues of miners marks her grave in the only union-owned cemetery in the United States.

Madam C.J. Walker (1867–1919)

Madam C.J. Walker, businesswoman, self-made millionaire, and philanthropist, was born Sarah Breedlove on December 23, 1867, in a leaky cabin on a cotton plantation in Delta, Louisiana. The daughter of former slaves, Walker developed hair care products and built her own factory. She provided employment to thousands of black women and was an important philanthropist. But, first, she had to overcome abject poverty and severe racial prejudice and discrimination.

Child laborer By the age of five, Sarah was working in the cotton fields with her family. She also helped her mother and sister Louvenia when they washed clothes for their family or did white people's laundry to earn money. From dawn to sundown, Sarah worked long and hard hours. When she was 7 years old, her parents died of yellow fever, a disease carried by mosquitoes. Sarah, Louvenia, and their brother Alex tried to support themselves and stay together. But, before long, Alex left to try to find a job in the city of Vicksburg, Mississippi. Soon, Sarah and Louvenia

Opposite: This monument to Mary Harris "Mother" Jones was erected in the Union Miners Cemetery, Mt. Olive, Illinois, in 1936.

Below: Young Sarah Breedlove had to work hard even when she was only 5 years old.

followed him there. Vicksburg had a large population with a lot of clothes to wash; so Sarah and Louvenia were able to support themselves.

When she was 14 years old, Sarah married Moses McWilliams. Three years later, she had a baby daughter, Lelia. Within two years of Lelia's birth, Sarah McWilliams' husband died, probably killed in a race riot in Greenwood, Mississippi, where he had gone to look for work.

Segregation It was a period in U.S. history of increasing violence and discrimination against black people. For about 10 years after the Civil War, the federal government tried to protect the rights of black people. But, in 1877, the president of the United States withdrew the last federal troops from Southern states. Many white Southerners joined secret racist organizations and terrorized black people by destroying their property, whipping them, and lynching them. A system of laws and customs that applied to schools, transportation, theaters, and parks was instituted in Southern states to segregate black people from white society.

McWilliams had heard that there was less violence and discrimination against black people in St. Louis, Missouri. She had also heard that washerwomen made more money there. Determined to make it on her own, McWilliams decided to move to St. Louis. "I had to make my own living and my own opportunity," she once said.

McWilliams worked hard in St. Louis. She became part of a growing and thriving black community. Through her church activities, she met black doctors, lawyers, and business people, who were well educated and well dressed. Determined to improve herself, McWilliams thought a lot about her situation. "But with all my thinking, I couldn't see how I, a poor washerwoman, was going to better my condition," she later explained.

> **"I am endeavoring to provide employment for hundreds of the women of my race."**
> —*Madam C.J. Walker*

Hair care products About 1905, McWilliams developed a hair product to use on her hair because it was brittle and broken and falling out in spots. According to her, "He (God) answered my prayers, for one night I had a dream, and in that dream a big black man appeared to me and told me what to mix up for my hair. Some of the remedy was grown in Africa, but I sent for it, mixed it, put it on my scalp, and in a few weeks my hair was coming in faster than it had ever fallen out."

McWilliams relocated to Denver, Colorado, where she began selling her products door-to-door. She also

Madam C.J. Walker was an attractive young woman with strong features.

perfected three products—Wonderful Hair Grower, Glossine, and Vegetable Shampoo—and redesigned a steel comb with wider gaps between the teeth to use with the thick, tightly curled hair of most black people. Her customers loved her products immediately. Charles Joseph Walker, an old friend from St. Louis, moved to Denver and gave her advice about advertising and promotion. In 1906, they got married and Sarah started using the name Madam C.J. Walker.

Promoting her products Madam Walker traveled extensively selling her products. She opened beauty parlors and founded Lelia College, a school for training people in the Walker Hair Care Method. In 1910, she settled in Indianapolis, Indiana, and started a beauty school and a laboratory, and built a factory. Two years later, Walker attended the all-male National Negro Business League convention. When the president ignored her efforts to speak, Walker stood up in the audience and said, "Surely you are not going to shut the door in my face. ...I am a woman who came from the cotton fields of the South. I was promoted from there to the washtub. Then I was promoted to the cook kitchen, and from there I promoted myself into the business of manufacturing hair goods and preparations. I have built my own factory on my own ground."

Harlem, New York, was fast becoming a center for black intellectuals at the beginning of this century.

The Harlem crowd In 1913, Walker's daughter opened a beauty salon in a section of New York City now known as Harlem. Three years later, Madam Walker moved there, too. Harlem was an exciting place to be. A huge migration of black people from the rural South to cities of the North had just begun. Known as the Great Migration, this shift in population would continue throughout the 1920s. Black poets, writers, artists, and musicians were settling in Harlem. Businesses owned by black people were thriving. Harlem was the focus of a new spirit of race consciousness and pride. Walker provided indispensable financial support for a number of black artists and writers who were beginning to produce their works during this period called the Harlem Renaissance. Walker also gave money to many schools and organizations, including the National Association for the Advancement of Colored People, an organization founded in 1909 to "promote equality of rights and eradicate race prejudice among the citizens of the United States."

In 1918, Madam Walker moved into a 34-room mansion she had built in Irvington-on-Hudson, a small town of mostly wealthy white people not far from New York City. Called Villa Lewaro, Walker's mansion was the scene of many lavish parties. But health problems overcame Walker, and in 1919, at the age of 51, she died. According to her nurse, Walker's last words were: "I want to live to help my race."

Above: Madam C.J. Walker's 34-room mansion is being restored as a museum.

Eleanor Roosevelt (1884–1962)

In a recent survey of historians and other academics, Eleanor Roosevelt was ranked the most influential American woman of the 20th century. A first lady, diplomat, social activist, and author, Roosevelt was born Anna Eleanor in 1884, the daughter of upper-class Elliot and Anna Roosevelt. Both her parents had died by the time she was 10 years old, and Roosevelt went to live with her maternal grandmother. Her childhood was grim, and Roosevelt remembered herself as "a solemn child, without beauty." By all accounts, Roosevelt's youth was devoid of warmth and affection, except for the three years she spent at Allenswood, a private girls' school outside of London, England. There, the school's headmistress, Marie Souvestre, provided Roosevelt with warmth, affection, and a role model of an independent, outspoken woman. "Whatever I have become since had its seeds in those three years of contact with a liberal mind and strong personality," wrote Roosevelt.

Involvement in reform movements In 1905 Eleanor Roosevelt married her distant cousin Franklin Delano Roosevelt (FDR). Between 1906 and 1916, she gave birth to six children. Roosevelt's mother-in-law dominated her home life, and she suffered from a deep sense of insecurity and inadequacy.

Nevertheless, she persevered and balanced her domestic responsibilities with her involvement in various reform organizations. Franklin became increasingly involved in politics, and, so did Eleanor.

After he was confined to a wheelchair, FDR *(below)* relied more and more on Eleanor *(opposite)* to be his spokesperson.

"I wish that Mrs. Roosevelt would stick to her knitting. …After all, the people did not elect her president."
—*a government official who resented her influence*

In 1918, she learned about FDR's affair with her social secretary, Lucy Mercer. "The bottom dropped out of my world. I faced myself, my surroundings, my world, honestly for the first time," Roosevelt told a friend. Although the Roosevelts reconciled, their marriage became more a practical partnership than an intimate relationship. Roosevelt steadfastly moved on, expanding her involvement in various causes and developing new emotional attachments to people such as Nancy Cook, Marion Dickerman, and Harry Hopkins.

In 1921, FDR was paralyzed by polio and confined to a wheelchair. In order to maintain his position as the leader of the Democratic party in New York State, FDR relied on his wife to be his representative and provide him with first-hand observations. Compelled by her profound commitment to social reform and women's issues, Roosevelt became an effective advocate. She spoke to innumerable groups, dictated hundreds of letters, and always reminded FDR about the needs of disadvantaged people.

First lady FDR was elected president of the United States in 1932, and again in 1936, 1940, and 1944. The longest-serving U.S. president, FDR's terms spanned The Great Depression and World War II. As first lady, Roosevelt used her position and influence to fight

A poster commemorating Eleanor Roosevelt's centennial in 1984.

ELEANOR ROOSEVELT CENTENNIAL 1884 - 1984

for the rights of women, the poor and working-class people, young people, and African-Americans. She gave weekly press conferences, wrote a syndicated newspaper column called *My Day*, and broadcast a radio show. An indefatigable traveler, Roosevelt toured the United States repeatedly. She visited relief projects and surveyed conditions in mines and factories. She urged FDR to support laws banning discrimination and to appoint black people and women to positions of authority. She acted as an advocate for Jewish war refugees.

Her story continues FDR died in 1945. "The story is over," she told a reporter not long after FDR's death. FDR's was; but there was to be a lot more to Eleanor Roosevelt's story. She became a U.S.

delegate to the United Nations and the prime force behind the Universal Declaration of Human Rights.

A beloved public figure, Roosevelt was a fierce advocate of civil rights, world peace, and the alleviation of human suffering. A worldwide traveler, Roosevelt became known as the first lady of the world.

Roosevelt died in 1962. In a tribute at her funeral, a friend said, "Because of her life, millions of others may have experienced a new sense of possibility. She would have wished for nothing more."

Helen Keller (1880–1968)

One of America's most famous women, Helen Keller was born without disabilities. However, at 19 months, she

> "Literature is my Utopia. Here I am not disenfranchised. No barrier of the senses shuts me out from the sweet gracious discourse of my book friends."
> —Helen Keller

became ill and lost her sight and hearing and consequently her ability to speak. According to Keller, until she was almost 5 years old, she was "wild and unruly, giggling and chuckling to express pleasure; kicking, scratching, uttering the choked screams of the deaf-mute to indicate the opposite."

Arrival of Anne Sullivan Shortly before Keller was 7 years old, Anne Sullivan became her teacher. Refusing to coddle or pity Keller, Sullivan set out to teach her manners, self-control, and independence. She also worked out a type of alphabet by which she spelled out words in Keller's hand. Once Keller made the connection between something she was feeling with one hand and the word Sullivan was spelling in her other hand (the first word she understood this way was *water*), she blossomed into a quick and eager student. She learned to read and write in Braille. By the time she was 16 years old, Keller could speak well enough to go to preparatory school. In 1904 she graduated with honors from Radcliffe College with studies in Greek, Latin,

Helen Keller as a teenager.

German, French, and English.

Keller and Sullivan, whom Keller called Teacher, stayed together until Sullivan's death in 1936. "Anne Sullivan Macy (her husband) was one of the pioneers in civilization for the blind and deaf. She saw the usefulness of whole souls in imperfect bodies," wrote Keller.

Working for the blind and deaf Helen Keller devoted her life to improving opportunities and conditions for blind and deaf-blind people. She testified before legislatures, lectured, wrote books and articles, and raised money. She spoke out against *ophthalmia*

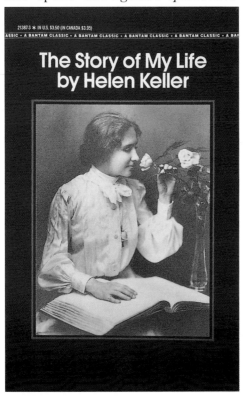

Helen Keller demonstrated that being blind and deaf need not confine disabled people to their own world. Using Braille, she could read and write a book.

213873 ✴ IN U.S. $3.50 (IN CANADA $3.95)
ASSIC · A BANTAM CLASSIC · A BANTAM CLASSIC · A BANTAM CLASSIC · A BANTAM CLASSIC · A BAI

**The Story of My Life
by Helen Keller**

neonatorum, the blindness of newborn infants caused by venereal disease in the mother, a subject that was not discussed in Keller's day until she broke the taboo. In 1909 she joined the Socialist Party. Undeterred by public reaction, Keller did not hesitate to identify herself as a "Socialist and Bolshevik" or as an opponent of child labor and capital punishment, and a supporter of suffrage, birth control, labor unions, and civil rights. "Many people have a wrong idea of what constitutes true happiness," Keller once wrote. "It is not attained through self-gratification but through fidelity to a worthy purpose."

"Look the world in the face" A tireless traveler, Keller lectured in more than 25 countries around the world. During World War II, she provided assistance and inspiration to soldiers who had been blinded in the war. "Never bend your head. Always hold it high. Look the world straight in the face," she counseled blind people. After the war she spoke in Hiroshima and Nagasaki, both devastated by atomic bombs, and was moved to resolve "to fight against the horrors of atomic warfare…"

During her lifetime, Keller received many awards, including the Chevalier's ribbon of the French Legion of Honor and the Alumni Achievement Award of Radcliffe College. Her books, including *The Story of My Life and Teacher,* have been translated into more than 50 languages and are sold worldwide. A movie was made about her life. Another movie, *The Miracle Worker,* which is also a play, tells the story of how Sullivan first made contact with Keller. A performance of *The Miracle Worker* is given each summer at Ivy Green, the birthplace of Keller in Tuscumbia, Alabama.

A teacher's achievement

Anne Sullivan started teaching Helen Keller on March 3, 1887, and made contact with her almost immediately. Keller's progress and Sullivan's achievement are evident in this letter written by Keller to her cousin Anna three and half months later:

"helen write anna george will give helen apple simpson will shoot bird jack will give helen stick of candy doctor will give mildred medicine mother will make mildred new dress"

Dolores Huerta (1930–)

"One thing I've learned as an organizer and activist is that having tremendous fears and anxieties is normal. It doesn't mean you should not do whatever is causing the anxiety; you should do it. By doing whatever causes your anxiety you overcome the fear and strengthen your emotional, spiritual, activist muscles. But if you give in to your fear, you will never develop the psychical strength you need," says Dolores Huerta, an activist and labor organizer.

A co-founder of the United Farm Workers Union in California, Huerta has demonstrated, organized, protested, and lobbied to improve working conditions for agricultural workers. She has organized strikes, led boycotts, and marched in support of various causes including pro-choice, the legal right of women to have an abortion. Huerta has been arrested at least 22 times. During one demonstration, she was beaten unconscious by police officers. "Women need women for energy. ...We can't wait for men to change the way they view us. We've got to make the changes and organize the pressure," Dolores Huerta says.

Born in 1930, the daughter of Juan and Alicia Fernandez, Huerta is a Chicana, an American woman of Mexican descent. Her parents were separated when she was 5 years old. With her mother, and her brothers and sister, Huerta moved to Stockton,

California, the center of the California canning industry, where her mother worked as a waitress and cannery worker. After saving enough money, Huerta's mother bought a restaurant and later a hotel.

Helping Chicanos After graduating from college, Huerta taught elementary school. Many of her students were the children of Chicano farm workers, who are the primary workers for the leading agricultural producers in California and other states in the southwestern United States. Following the various crop growing seasons, Chicano farm workers travel throughout the region, cultivating and harvesting the fruits and vegetables. They earn extremely low wages, live in substandard housing, and do not have health benefits or job security. Teaching the farm workers' children who were frequently hungry and without school supplies, decent clothing, or shoes made Huerta decide to be an organizer for the farm workers. In 1955, she joined the Community Service Organization, a group of people who worked to improve public services, pay, and living conditions for Chicanos. In 1962, she joined with Cesar Chavez to form the National Farm Workers Association. In

Farm workers, especially Chicanos, were the people Dolores Huerta and Cesar Chavez wanted to help when they set up the National Farm Workers Association in 1962.

¡SÍ, SE PÚEDE

DOLORES HUERTA
Labor Leader/Organizer

1965, *La Huelga* (*huelga* is the Spanish word for "strike"), a strike of grape harvesters, began. According to Huerta, "It was like a war, a daily kind of confrontation. We never slept. We'd get up at 3:00 or 4:00 a.m. and then we'd go till 11:00 p.m...." Huerta was in the thick of the action. In 1966 she negotiated the first contract with one group of employers. Four years later, the rest of the grape growers agreed to negotiate. "We accomplished a miracle!" says Huerta.

Huerta, who has been married several times, raised 11 children. "I always believed in involving them in everything I did," Huerta said. Although she was criticized for taking her children to picket lines and meetings, Huerta did not stop. Her children even went to jail with her.

Today Huerta is in her 60s, a respected grandmother, and still going strong because there is so much work to do. "As women we need so many different things on so many different levels—like the raising of self-esteem— so that women can think more of themselves and not be so easily dominated by men or outer authority," says Huerta. Clearly she has lived a life that is a powerful example for other women to follow.

Opposite: Dolores Huerta with Cesar Chavez.

Above: A poster in honor of Dolores Huerta. The slogan of the farm workers' struggles, "We can do it," is written in Spanish.

chapter six

A Lifetime

During her lifetime, a woman in the United States moves in and out of many stages. She fulfills many roles. Traditionally women were expected to move in set ways from birth through childhood, adolescence, courtship, marriage, motherhood, and old age to death. But the stages of a modern woman's life are not so predictable now. Labor-saving devices, the need for dual incomes to support families, abundant educational opportunities, increased longevity, and changing cultural mores are reshaping the stages in a woman's lifetime in the United States.

Birth and the girl child

Most babies in the United States are born in hospitals. Until the 1970s, fathers were excluded from the birth process. Today, however, many fathers play an active role by attending prenatal classes with pregnant wives, learning how to coach their wives in special breathing techniques, attending the birth, and cutting the umbilical cord.

Midwives and birthing centers are also becoming more popular now. Historically most babies in the United States were delivered by midwives. However, in the early 1900s, the newly-organized male medical profession succeeded in persuading the public that only physicians could attend childbirth. However, more and more women in the United States today are employing midwives in conjunction with doctors. Midwives charge considerably less money to attend a normal delivery. And, most

Opposite and right:
Women of all ages and from all walks of life in the United States are taking an active role in American society.

important to many parents, midwives focus on nurturing the laboring woman to give birth instead of just using technology and drugs, unless an emergency arises.

"Appropriate technology can be lifesaving and clearly has opened the doors for many more women to give birth. ...But these same technologies have cost consumers incredible amounts of money... By choosing a midwife (or one of the rare physicians who do practice the midwifery model), by taking responsibility for herself and her child, by saying "no" to certain technologies, by finding solutions that are not so intrusive and expensive, by educating herself about her health and her choices, a woman can turn things around," Jane Dwinell, a registered nurse and midwife, writes in her book, *Birth Stories*. In slowly growing numbers, women in the United States are agreeing with her.

Baby shower Many pregnant women are given a baby shower by their mother or close women friends. Sometimes it's a

State-of-the-art delivery room.

surprise party where the unsuspecting pregnant woman is greeted by a group of women friends bearing gifts. Whether a baby shower is an elaborate affair or simple, it is characterized by a lot of hugging, laughing, and celebrating. Gifts might include hand-knit sweaters, clothes, toys, a crib, books, a drinking cup, and a silver frame for the baby's photograph.

Historically, boy babies were valued more than girl babies; not necessarily loved more, but valued more because they were viewed as stronger and smarter than girls. Boys also carried on the father's surname and had access to education, wealth, and power. As late as 1902, researchers believed that intelligence was related to brain size and that males routinely had larger brains than women. This notion was finally dispelled when a female researcher compared the difference between the skull sizes of a group of male scientists and female college students and discovered that several women came out ahead of the men. In fact, the smallest skull belonged to a famous male scientist!

Sex differentiation Today most parents are careful not to appear to prefer a boy baby. But, from the moment a baby's sex is known, she or he is treated differently. How different is influenced by the parents' religious beliefs, racial and ethnic background, and education.

Today's mother sees herself as an educator as well as a caregiver.

For example, many highly educated professional parents work hard to avoid female/male stereotypes. However, at best, they can only tone them down because sex role stereotypes still abound in the culture. Boys are assumed to be more physically active, competitive, and naturally good at math. They supposedly prefer footballs and guns. Girls are thought to be naturally good at relationships, concerned about pleasing people, and cooperative. They supposedly prefer dolls and tea sets.

Newborn girl babies are identified by the hospital staff with pink—a blanket, a cap, a ribbon, a name tag. Boy babies with blue. Many parents, relatives, and friends will continue the pink/girl, blue/boy theme in clothes, room decorations, and gifts. Studies have shown that girl babies are held more often than boy babies. Adults also display a wider range of emotional

Four generations of women—great grandmother, grandmother, mother, and baby girl—enjoy a day out together.

responses to girl babies than to boys.

A generation ago, the baby would routinely be given the father's surname, the last name borne in common by all members of the same family. The boy baby would carry this surname for life, but the girl baby would eventually get married and take her husband's surname. Today, some newborn babies get a hyphenated or combined version of the parents' names or a new name altogether for a surname. In some cases, the parents give the mother's surname to a girl baby and the father's surname to a boy baby.

Childhood

The female/male stereotyping continues in childhood. If the child is a boy, the social programming is comparatively open-ended: he learns that he can do almost anything and is offered a wide choice of activities. If the child is a girl, she learns that girls have certain fixed roles and is prepared for female activities: sexual partner, wife, mother."

Studies have shown that girls are encouraged to think about how their actions affect other people, boys aren't. The messages boys hear include, "Big boys don't cry," and "What do you want to be when you grow up?" Girls hear, "Ladies don't shout," and "Do you have a boyfriend yet?"

Girls who shun dolls and play rough like boys are called tomboys. At an early age, many girls start using makeup and wearing sexually provocative clothes. According to researchers Nancy Frazier and Myra Sadker, "For girls, as they are molded into roles of women, there is a concomitant ebbing away of pride and self-esteem. The loss of dignity, the growing feelings of inferiority that come from being made female have been documented in numerous studies." A 1990 study, *Shortchanging Girls, Shortchanging America*, documents a loss of self-confidence in girls that is twice that for boys as they move from childhood to adolescence.

A growing number of adults are trying to counter the female/male stereotypes. Linda Stockdale, an attorney and grandmother, recently created Career Pals, new dolls for girls. Representing a range of ethnic groups, Career Pals are dressed to represent 26 professions as role models for little girls. When their twin daughters were nine years old, Nancy Gruver and Joe Kelly decided to

Girls Incorporated gives girls the opportunity to do nontraditional activities. The girls in the picture below are taking apart an iron to see how it works.

As they grow up, girls tend to become more shy and inhibited in the classroom.

start a new magazine for girls, *New Moon: The Magazine for Girls and Their Dreams.* "A lot of people my age who have daughters are learning that things haven't changed enough since we were adolescents," says Gruver, who is determined to offer new images and messages.

Adolescence

The teenage girl is often embarrassed by her body as it undergoes the physiological changes set off by her newly activated sex hormones. Her breasts start to develop, hair appears in new places, and menstruation begins. In the American culture that idealizes the extremes of female bodies—the big-busted, blond movie star or the skinny, flat-chested model—an adolescent girl may fear that she is too tall or too short, too thin or too fat, too flat-chested or too big-busted. She worries about the shape of her nose and the appearance of pimples on her face. Many adolescent girls dread "bad hair" days, a day when their hair won't stay in place. Plagued by a negative image of their bodies, all too many adolescent girls in the United States develop serious eating disorders. Adolescent girls attempt suicide four to five times as often as boys; however, boys, who choose more lethal methods, are more likely to die.

> "A girl should not expect special privileges because of her sex but neither should she adjust to prejudice and discrimination."
> —*Betty Friedan, author and activist*

Dating and being "cool" Many adolescent girls get caught up in the pressure to please boys and date. They also feel pressure to "be cool," which can mean everything from idolizing a particular singing group, dressing in the current fashion, to using the current words and expressions. With the widespread availability of birth control information and devices and changing moral standards, girls are becoming sexually active at much earlier ages than in previous generations. As they grow up, adolescent girls increase their sexual activity: 27% of 15-year-olds have had intercourse at least once, 34% of 16-year-olds, 51% of 17-year-olds, and 70% of 18-year-olds.

The United States has the highest rate of teenage childbearing in the Western industrialized world. Today one out of every six babies in the United States is born to an adolescent mother.

Friends become very important to adolescent girls. They talk on the telephone and go shopping together. In larger numbers than boys, girls come together to campaign against drunk driving and drug abuse, work to protect the environment, raise money for AIDS

These two girls are looking at a museum display on myths about women.

research, and volunteer to help people with disabilities. As adults, females continue to be more altruistic than men according to a recent study that found that two-thirds of women aged 25 to 40 volunteered their time compared to about half of the men surveyed.

Many grassroots organizations are organizing to provide support and services for adolescent girls. The Aroostook Micmac Council in Presque Isle, Maine, was established in 1982 to provide services for the Micmac Indians. The Council is developing a "traditional" girls council to help build girls' self-esteem and offer them broader options for the future. Girls attend monthly classes on family planning, birth control, job planning, and date rape. Medicine women instruct girls about Micmac traditions, women's tribal roles, and the importance of delaying marriage.

The Art of Living in New York City is an educational interarts performance collective with programs designed to promote self-esteem in adolescent Latinas and prevent teen sexual abuse. Latina girls between the ages of 11 and 14 explore gender issues that affect their lives, learn leadership skills, and participate in projects that develop their self-esteem.

"Growing up is serious business" is

Coming-of-age ceremonies

Different geographic areas and subcultures have a variety of different ceremonies to mark a girl's entry into womanhood, including debutante balls for upper-class girls in which they are formally introduced to society and eligible men, sweet 16 parties in which peers celebrate a girl's 16th birthday with loud music and dancing, and *quinceanara* celebrations for Hispanic girls on their 15th birthday that are announced by elegant invitations and involve many family members and friends, lots of food, and the birthday girl wearing a fancy, frilly dress. *Bat mitzvah,* a celebration for 13-year-old Jewish girls, is becoming more widely practiced by a group that has by and large reserved its rituals and celebrations for males. The invitation card featured here was sent out by Miriam Julia Skurnick and her parents for her *bat mitzvah.* During the service, Miriam said, "I am a feminist."

Left and below: At any age, girls treasure the friendship and company of other girls.

the motto of Girls, Incorporated, a nationwide network of over 300 centers located in 135 cities across the United States. The majority of centers are located in low-income areas and provide a weekly average of 30 hours of after-school, weekend, and summer activities. "We know how prejudice, stereotyping, and society's low expectations have held girls back," says Margaret Gates, executive director of Girls, Inc. "As women, we need to pave the way for the next generation of women because society isn't going to do it for us; we have to do it for each other," says Mary B. Daly, M.D., Ph.D., who attended Girls, Inc. when she was an adolescent.

Graduation from high school is an important stage in a girl's life.

Education

Today public school education is free and available to all children in the United States from kindergarten through high school for a total of 13 years. Since 1970, increasing numbers of women have obtained high school diplomas. From 1970 to 1989, the number of white women high school graduates went from 55% to 78.2%; the number of black women graduates went from 32.6% to 65%; and the number of Hispanic women graduates went from 30.9% to 50.8%. At the college and university level, more women than men are now attending college. The number of women attending the U.S. military service academies has also increased. In 1991, 13.6% from the graduating class of the U.S. Air Force Academy were women; 10.2% from the Coast Guard Academy; 9.7% from West Point, the Military Academy; and 8.6% from Annapolis, the Naval Academy.

Despite these gains, recent studies document the fact that sex discrimination still pervades all areas of education in the United States. According to *The AAUW Report: How Schools Shortchange Girls*, teachers call on girls less often than boys and praise girls for good behavior and neatness rather than academic performance; girls are discouraged from taking math and science; and textbooks frequently ignore or stereotype the experiences of girls and women. African-American girls have fewer interactions with teachers than do white girls, despite evidence that they attempt to initiate interactions more frequently. Research shows a tendency, beginning at the preschool level, for educators to choose classroom activities that appeal to boys' interests and to select presentation formats in which boys excel. Reports of boys sexually harassing girls in schools are increasing. A recent survey revealed that 81% of students have experienced sexual harassment at school, including having their breasts grabbed, buttocks pinched, and enduring sexual taunts and name-calling.

"The wealth of statistical evidence must convince even the most skeptical that gender bias in our schools is shortchanging girls—and compromising our country," writes Alice McKee, president of the American Association of University Women Educational Foundation. In late 1993, the Gender Equity in Education Package was introduced in the U.S. Senate that proposes education reforms such as: training to help teachers eliminate classroom practices that diminish girls' academic abilities and confidence; recruiting female math and science teachers in order to build a corps of role models for girls; providing training and technical assistance to combat sexual harassment; and identifying and developing programs that address bias against girls and women in education.

Mary Hatwood Futrell is a leading educator in the United States. A former president of the National Education Association, Futrell is currently president of The World Confederation for Organizations of Teaching.

Maya Ying Lin, an architect and the daughter of Chinese emigres, designed the Civil Rights Memorial at the Southern Law Center in 1989.

Career

For generations, middle- and upper-class women in the United States were brought up to be wives and mothers. If they went to college, it was to "catch a man," to get a "Mrs." degree, the title signifying a married woman. If these women thought of doing paid work, it was in terms of jobs they might do to earn spending money to supplement their husband's income or to buy extras for the family, or something they might do when the children started school.

Until the mid-1960s, most middle- and upper-class married women accepted without question that their primary job was to take care of a husband and children. Of course, working-class women never had that option. Although they, too, were raised to "catch" a man, get married, and have children, they also had to have jobs that inevitably came with low pay, low status, and no possibility for promotion.

Working for a living Although many young women today still want to get married and have children, they have very different attitudes toward earning money. Most women know that now it generally takes two incomes for a family to maintain a good standard of living in the United States. They also know that they will spend fewer years as active mothers because they will have fewer children than their mothers did. Older women who were raised with the traditional model have learned some hard lessons because of the difficult economy and rising divorce rate. Currently one out of two marriages ends in divorce.

There are many women who choose to remain single. And, a growing number of women who are choosing to have children without getting married, juggling a career and the demands of single parenthood. With the change in conditions, expectations, and opportunities, careers are something women today think about, plan for, and work hard in to achieve success.

During the last decades, women in the United States have developed a variety of career patterns. Some women get their training and start a career before they start a family. Once they have children, these women continue to work and make a variety of child care arrangements. Other women are in and out of their career as they take breaks to devote themselves to their children. Other women start their career after their children start kindergarten, or even later when their children are grown.

Regardless of the pattern they follow, women face many problems. At home, they do the bulk of the domestic work.

"Women still have the primary responsibility for children and housekeeping, spending twice as much time on these chores than their professional husbands," says Sandra Day O'Connor, the first woman member of the U.S. Supreme Court. At work, they face subtle and not so subtle discrimination including sexual harassment.

Today women have careers in a variety of fields. Although they are still concentrated in traditionally female careers such as nursing, education, and secretarial work, women have made dramatic inroads into nontraditional fields including the Army, Navy, Air Force, and Marine Corps. Barely visible in the U.S. military in the early 1970s,

The military, traditionally thought to be a male domain, is now recruiting more and more women.

Architects Ann Marshall *(left)* and Rae Kinoshita *(right)* sign autographs for admirers at the dedication ceremonies of a historical park that they designed.

Courtship and marriage

Until the late 1960s, dating and courtship was very predictable in the United States; typically young men and women were introduced to each other by friends and family, then the young man asked the young woman out, picked her up, took her to the event, and paid for everything. Couples typically got formally engaged for a period of time before getting married.

Today courtship in the United States is no longer that predictable. Courtships can begin in various ways: through friends, a casual meeting at work or school, and by signing up for a dating

women now appear in significant numbers. Notable numbers of women of color serve in the military.

In 1992, according to officials, black women made up 48.7% of all women in the Army's enlisted ranks, and 20.2% of all the Army's women officers; 26.8% of the Navy's enlisted women; 28.5% of the Marine Corps' enlisted women and 23.7% of the Air Force. Latina, Native American, and Asian-American women were also represented. Women are also building careers as professional athletes. Julie Krone has compiled an impressive record as a top jockey, Lynn St. James is a champion race car driver, and Martina Navratilova is an international tennis star.

Sexual harassment

A matter of widespread concern in the U.S., sexual harassment is generally viewed as uninvited and unwanted attention, including letters, telephone calls or materials of a sexual nature; touching; sexually suggestive looks or gestures; pressure for sexual favors or dates; sexual jokes or questions; actual or attempted assault, or rape. In response to legislation and law suits, companies, businesses, and institutions are developing strategies and programs to eliminate sexual harassment.

Lonely hearts corner

A sample of advertisements by women in a recent newspaper includes: "I want the real thing. I'm a tall, slim and attractive white Christian female, 38 years old, who wishes to meet a tall, sincere gentleman. If any or perhaps all the above describes you, I await your call so that we may talk further; Fullfigured single black professional woman, 40, seeks white or Hispanic gentleman for relationship. Age 55-late 60s. No drugs or disease; Blue-eyes, Italian-American, 35, slim, Catholic, nice looking too! Seeking sincere, good-looking Italian American guy for serious relationship. Must be slim, tall or medium height. Drug and disease free, nonsmoker preferred; Latin Educated in Europe. Green eyes, blond hair, divorced, 40s looks 35. Passionate, sincere, people person, caring, open, smart, parent of two kids. Marriage minded. Someone with clean life and mind please; Genuinely nice Jewish female, 30, nonsmoker. Fun, attractive, intelligent, hopeless, romantic. Seeks tall white male for fun, romance, and forever."

service that matches people according to their interests. Women and men take compatibility tests, make videotapes, and join singles clubs. They also take out advertisements in newspapers and magazines.

Once the courtship begins, couples go out on dates, talk on the telephone, write letters, and exchange gifts. American advertisers are always exhorting men to court women with roses, chocolates, and diamonds. On Valentine's Day, lovers and friends express their love by exchanging greeting cards, bouquets of flowers, and boxes of candy. At some point, a couple may decide to live together without getting married. At one time this was considered scandalous, but today "living together" has become a common practice.

Women who do choose to get married participate in a plethora of rituals many of which are now being adapted to fit nontraditional ideas. Traditionally, the man or groom-to-be had to ask the woman's father for permission to marry his daughter. If this is done today, it is usually done as a courtesy and sometimes both her parents are asked, not just the father. In addition, some women return the courtesy and ask the man's parents for their permission. Before the wedding, many women wear a diamond engagement ring, a gift from the man.

The wedding The woman will attend many showers given by her mother, female relatives, and female friends. Some showers are elegant parties with music and food. Others are simple with snacks and drinks. Typical shower gifts include lacy lingerie, photograph albums, and household items. The bride-to-be carefully opens each gift and passes it around for everyone to admire.

Considerable time and money are spent selecting a wedding dress and special dresses for the bridesmaids, friends of the bride who will participate in the wedding ceremony. A traditional wedding dress is a white, lacy gown with a long train and a veil. The color white and the veil are symbols of virginity. Most weddings are held in churches and synagogues with a religious leader officiating, even when the couple is not religious. Other weddings take place in parks, backyards, and city halls. Couples have also gotten married while parachuting out of airplanes, scuba diving, standing on a mountain top, and on a nude beach along the Atlantic Ocean.

Many women, and men more often now, wear wedding rings on the third finger of the left hand. The third finger was selected because it was thought that there was a vein in the third finger that ran directly to the heart. Few people know that historically men put the ring on their left hand because it was considered weaker than the right. They also probably do not know that the tradition of having the father escort the bride to the groom at the beginning of the wedding ceremony originally signified the legal transfer of the bride from her father to her husband.

Typically the bride assumed her groom's surname as her own and used the title of "Mrs." Today many couples handle the name-change tradition in a variety of ways: they keep their own name, they hyphenate their surnames, or they create a new surname. Although some women use "Mrs." (most notably President Clinton's wife Hillary), many married and unmarried women use the

title "Ms.," which does not reveal marital status.

Traditionally marriage was the only respectable avenue to having a family in the United States. Married couples receive many benefits including formal societal recognition of their relationship and legal protection such as the right to share various insurance and pension plans and, in some cases, the benefit of special income tax exemptions. While unmarried couples may receive benefits, they are not guaranteed. Today, people in the United States are increasingly choosing other ways to form partnerships and have families. In the 1990s, a record number of women who have never married are adopting children or giving birth without making a permanent commitment to a man. In addition, there is increasing acceptance of gay and lesbian adoptions and more children are finding homes in their households.

Motherhood

The word motherhood conjures up many images, most of them far from the realities of real mother's lives. In general, mothers in the United States have been either idealized or vilified. They have been portrayed as manipulative

A 19th-century Valentine card.

Being a mother in the 20th century means juggling a career, childrearing duties, and household responsibilities.

monsters or self-effacing, self-sacrificing saints. According to novels, movies, magazines, and psychiatrists, there are bad mothers who breed children with severe psychological problems or good mothers full of love and wise counsel. There are mothers who are torn between the family and their career. Mothers who drive their children to murder. Mothers who emasculate their husbands and sons. Mothers who are guilty of coldness, rejection, hysteria, smothering, controlling, and mania.

While these old images still linger, mothers in the United States today are being redefined as fully human, multi-dimensional women who are doing their best to handle a complex and challenging role. Women become mothers for a variety of reasons: societal expectations, religious prohibitions against birth control, confirming femininity, fulfilling a happy marriage, distraction from an unhappy marriage,

personal fulfillment, companionship, boredom, or a desire to perpetuate a family. In addition, a wider variety of women are becoming mothers in the United States. With technological advances that reduce the risks, notable numbers of women in their late 30s and 40s are becoming mothers for the first time. As their rights are being more widely recognized, more lesbians are becoming mothers. So are women who are choosing to remain single.

Modern mothers have more formal education than previous generations, and access to a variety of resources, information, and organizations. Mothers in the United States read about childbirth and child rearing, attend prenatal classes with their partners, learn special exercises and breathing techniques to reduce the pain of labor, and involve their partners as helpmates through labor and delivery. They debate the pros and cons of breast-feeding, the often contradictory advice about how to raise children, and the pluses and minuses of combining paid work with motherhood. Of course, many women do not have a choice about whether or not they should earn a salary. They have to. More than a quarter of all American families are now headed by one parent, usually the mother. Other mothers continue their careers for self-fulfillment. In 1991, 58% of all mothers with children under 6 years old were in the labor force.

Mother's Day

Motherhood is celebrated in the United States on Mother's Day, the second Sunday of May. Anna M. Jarvis, an unmarried teacher from Philadelphia, Pennsylvania, is credited with launching the idea some years after the death of her own mother. Devoted to her mother, Jarvis conducted a massive letter-writing crusade to promote the idea of once a year setting aside a day to remember mothers. Originally conceived as a religious holiday, the first Mother's Day was celebrated in 1872. At that time, Jarvis started the tradition of wearing a pink carnation in honor of a living mother and a white carnation in honor of a dead mother. Jarvis's idea caught on and by 1912 Mother's Day was officially observed in every state. In 1914, President Woodrow Wilson officially proclaimed the second Sunday in May as Mother's Day throughout the United States. According to Wilson, Mother's Day is "a public expression of our love and reverence for the mothers of this country."

Mother's Day quickly became highly commercial with card companies, candy manufacturers, and gift manufacturers waging huge advertising campaigns to sell their wares. Restaurants offer special Mother's Day menus, and, for years, Mother's Day has been the busiest day of the year in the restaurant business.

Opposite: Standing beside her husband, Kate Nunn happily holds baby William, whom she and her husband adopted as a newborn.

The National Women's History Project's card features a quilt based on drawings made by American and Soviet children. Quilted by American and Soviet mothers, it is a symbol of the unity of mothers committed to a peaceful future for their children.

A meaningful Mother's Day In a desire to make Mother's Day mean more than the temporary pleasure of candy and flowers, The National Women's History Project offers Mother's Day gift cards that help promote the rediscovery of women's history in schools and communities throughout the United States. The inside of the card reads: "Throughout our history, in thousands of ways, women have given love, support, dedication, and inspirations to

> **"What is sad for women of my generation is that they weren't supposed to work if they had families. What were they to do when the children were grown—watch the raindrops coming down the window-pane?"**
> —*Jacqueline Kennedy Onassis, former first lady and editor*

their families and their communities to help build a better tomorrow for us all. Your contribution to the precious fabric of women's history has not gone unnoticed. In your name, I have made a Mother's Day contribution to the National Women's History Project. This gift will help carry forth the important work of writing women back into our nation's history. Women's history recognizes and remembers women like you who have touched and inspired many generations."

Old age

Perhaps because the United States is a young country, youth is idealized. Old age is a stage many Americans go to great lengths to forestall, transcend, or deny. Plastic surgery is a billion-dollar business. So are health clubs, physical fitness centers, and dieting programs. Gray hair is dyed. Wrinkles are smoothed away with creams, massages, and the surgeon's knife. However, with

increased longevity and the inevitable aging of the generation of baby boomers, people born between 1946 and 1964 who constituted the largest segment of the U.S. population, Americans are slowly beginning to shift their attention to old age.

In 1988, the life expectancy of women was 78.9 years, seven years longer than men. In 1993, Americans past the age of 85, a group that gerontologists call the "old old," were the fastest growing group in the United States. Maggie Kuhn, founder of the Gray Panthers, an advocacy group for elderly people, is now one of the "old old." A pioneer spokesperson on issues of aging such as medical economics, health patterns and ailments of older women, problems of addiction, financial concerns, lifelong sexuality, and housing, Kuhn talks about positive aspects of aging, "I think it is easier to have hope when one is very old. One sees that over the course of time, people have managed to overcome countless difficulties with amazing resourcefulness."

According to older women, friendships with other women are extremely important to them.

Life does not end when one grows old. Older women can take part in any of a number of activities such as quilting *(above)* or even go "trick-or-treating" at Halloween with their granddaughter *(opposite)*.

widowed. In addition to adjusting to life alone, widows frequently experience a reduction in income.

One out of five women over the age of 65 lives in poverty. According to one economist, "If you're a woman, you have a 60% shot at being poor in old age." Women aged 65 and older are twice as likely as men to be poor.

Nevertheless, most older women in the United States hold on to their creativity, courage, resilience, and determination to live a meaningful life. "But I have learned to calm many of my fears about aging by simplifying my life, by learning to enjoy my solitude, by redefining my definition of success, by valuing my friendships with women, by cultivating my inner life through a spiritual connection to nature and creative expression, and by trying my best to be alive in the present moment," Cathleen Rountree writes in her book, *On Women Turning 50: Celebrating Mid-Life Discoveries*.

According to Kuhn, "The elderly lobby has been forceful and effective in preserving benefits for the old. I would like to see it speak out as powerfully on behalf of the nearly 14 million children who now constitute 40% of the nation's poor…the old must not simply advocate on their own behalf. We must act as elders of the tribe, looking out for the best interests of the future and preserving the precious compact between the generations."

Like Kuhn, many older women are finding ways to remain active and positive in their old age. They are shedding the traditional stereotype of old women in the United States as shriveled up, sexless, without meaning beyond their childbearing years, depressed, doddering, and dimwitted. In fact, many women are finding that aging is liberating. They are free from the demands of raising children. Free from the possibility of unwanted pregnancy. Free from the pressure of trying to emulate the skinny, smooth-skinned, pubescent image of femininity.

However, despite the freedom they may feel, many women face serious problems in their old age. By age 65, half of all American women are

Women's Firsts

Susan B. Anthony

(1820–1906) When the U.S. Treasury began circulating the Susan B. Anthony one-dollar coin in 1979, she became the first woman pictured on a U.S. coin. A major leader of the 19th-century woman suffrage movement, she believed that "Failure is impossible."

Elizabeth Blackwell

(1821–1910) In 1849, she became the first woman to receive a medical degree from a U.S. medical school. Despite being the object of ridicule and scorn, she graduated at the top of her class. She later founded a highly regarded medical college.

Pearl Buck

(1892–1973) In 1938, she became the first American woman to win a Nobel Prize for Literature. She wrote over 100 books including *The Good Earth*, a novel based on her experiences living in China, and *The Child Who Never Grew*, about her daughter who was mentally retarded.

Bessie Coleman

(1893–1926) Because she was black, she was not allowed to learn to fly in the United States. So, she went to France to learn. In 1921, she became the first American woman to earn an international pilot's license. She returned to America and was a celebrity until she died in an accident.

Grace Murray Hopper

(1906–1992) A computer pioneer, she was the first person to develop the concept of automatic programming (1951), the first woman to receive the Computer Science Man-of-the-Year award from the Data Processing Management Association (1969), the first woman named a Distinguished Fellow of the British Computer Society, the first woman admiral in the U.S. Navy, and the first individual to be awarded the U.S. Medal of Technology (1991).

Wilma Mankiller

(b. 1945) In 1987, she was elected the first woman chief of the 108,000-member Cherokee Nation, the second largest Native American tribe.

Frances Perkins

(1880–1965) In 1933, she became the first woman member in a U.S. president's cabinet. She served as secretary of labor for an unprecedented 12 years. During Perkins's tenure, laws were passed that set minimum wages, maximum hours, abolished child labor, established unemployment insurance and social security.

Jeannette Rankin

(1880–1973) In 1916, four years before women won the right to vote throughout the United States, voters in the state of Montana elected her to the House of Representatives, making her the first woman to serve in the U.S. Congress. A life-long pacifist, she was the first and only member of Congress to vote against entering World War II.

Vinnie Ream	(1847–1914) In 1866, she became the first woman sculptor to win a federal commission for a sculpture. Her task was to produce a marble sculpture of President Abraham Lincoln, who had been assassinated in 1865. The sculpture is in the rotunda of the U.S. Capitol.
Anna Eleanor Roosevelt	(1884–1962) A social activist and prolific writer, she was the wife of President Franklin D. Roosevelt. She was the first U.S. president's wife to hold a press conference (1933), to travel by air to a foreign country (1934), and, as former first lady, to be appointed delegate to the United Nations (1945).
Wilma Rudolph	(b. 1940) She wore a heavy leg brace until she was 12 years old. But, with the help of her family, she built up her strength until she was a champion athlete. In 1960, she became the first woman runner to win three gold medals at a single Olympics, the first to win both Olympic sprint events, and the first to win an Olympic 200-meter dash.
Florence Sabin	(1871–1953) A medical doctor and researcher, she discovered keys to how the human lymphatic system works. In 1919 she discovered the origin of red corpuscles. In 1925, she became the first woman member of the National Academy of Sciences.
Deborah Sampson (Gannett)	(1760–1827) During the American Revolutionary War, she was the first woman to disguise herself as a man and fight in battle. During medical treatment for an illness, her true identity was discovered and she was discharged. She then became the first woman to earn money giving lectures in her uniform about her military experience.
Elizabeth Cochrane Seaman (known as Nellie Bly)	(1867–1922) In 1889, this famous newspaper reporter traveled by steamship, train, and rickshaw and became the first person to circle the globe alone in 72 days, six hours, 11 minutes, and 14 seconds.
Maggie Lena Walker	(1867–1934) In 1903, she established the St. Luke Penny Savings Bank in Richmond, Virginia, and became the first woman bank president.
Frances Willard	(1839–1898) Her motto was "Do Everything." In 1871, she became the first woman college president. In 1905 she became the first woman to have her statue in Statuary Hall in the U.S. Capitol where it still stands.
Ellen Taafe Zwilich	(b. 1939) In 1975, she became the first woman to receive her doctorate in composition from the top-ranked Julliard School in New York City. In 1983 she became the first woman to win the prestigious Pulitzer Prize for music.

Glossary

America	The name used to mean the United States or the two continents—North and South America. It first appeared on a map in 1507 in honor of Italian explorer Amerigo Vespucci, who had explored the coast of South America.
Cabinet	The President's official advisers.
Congress	The legislative branch of the U.S. federal government that consists of two houses, the Senate and the House of Representatives. Congress has the power to enact, revise, and repeal laws, to assess and collect taxes, to regulate interstate and foreign commerce, to coin money, to establish post offices, to maintain the armed forces, and to declare war.
Constitution	The fundamental rules of government which defines the rights of citizens and of states and the structure and powers of the federal government.
Declaration of Independence	The document adopted on July 4, 1776, in which representatives of the 13 American colonies asserted their independence from Great Britain.
feminism	A theory based on the legal, economic, and social equality of women and men.
indentured servants	People who agreed to work without pay for a certain period of time, usually, five to seven years, to pay the costs of their transportation to America.
labor force	An available supply of workers.
ratification	To make legal by official approval.
suffrage	The right of voting.
unconstitutional	Not permitted by the Constitution.
United States of America	Also called America, the U.S., the U.S.A., or the United States. Made up of 50 states, the United States is the world's third largest country after Canada and China. The federal capital is in Washington, D.C. (District of Columbia).

Further Reading

Davis, Flora: *Moving the Mountain: The Women's Movement in America Since 1960*, Simon & Schuster, New York, 1991.

Dubois, Ellen Carol, and Ruiz, Vicki L., eds.: *Unequal Sisters: A Multicultural Reader in U.S. Women's History*, Routledge, New York, 1990.

Evans, Sara M.: *Born for Liberty: A History of Women in America*, Free Press, New York, 1989.

Faladi, Susan: *Backlash*, Crown Publishers, New York, 1991.

Flexner, Eleanor: *Century of Struggle*, Atheneum, New York, 1974.

Friedan, Betty: *The Feminine Mystique*, Dell Pub. Co., New York, 1963.

Giddings, Paula: *When and Where I Enter: The Impact of Black Women on Race and Sex in America*, Bantam Books, New York, 1984.

Green, Rayna: *Women in American Indian Society*, Chelsea House, New York, 1992.

Hymnowitz, Carol, and Weissman, Michael: *A History of Women in America*, Bantam Books, New York, 1978.

James, Edward T., Wilson James, Janet, and Boyers, Paul S., eds.: *Notable American Women: A Biographical Dictionary 3 Volumes*, Belknap Press, Cambridge, Massachusetts, 1971.

Rappaport, Doreen: *American Women Their Lives in Their Words*, Harper Collins, New York, 1990.

Read, Phyllis J., and Witlieb, Bernard L.: *The Book of Women's Firsts: Breakthrough Achievements of Almost 1,000 American Women*, Random House, New York, 1992.

Werthelmer, Barbara Meyer: *We Were There: The Story of Working Women in America*, Pantheon, New York, 1977.

Yung, Judy: *Chinese Women of America: A Pictorial History*, University of Washington Press, Seattle, Washington, 1986.

Picture Credits

American Association of University Women: 50
Associated Press: 89
Penny Colman: 3, 4, 5, 8, 19, 20, 26, 27, 34, 35, 36, 38, 40, 41, 46, 55, 62, 63, 64, 68, 71, 73, 78, 87, 90, 98, 99, 102, 105, 106, 108, 112, 114, 116, 121, 122, 123
Consolidated Edison Company of New York: 61
Culver Pictures: 9, 14, 16, 18, 21, 24, 28, 30, 31, 49, 76
DDB Stock Photo (Inga Spence): 95
Dollywood Foundation: 51
Girls, Incorporated: 103
Linda Hickson: 65, 107
Holy Name Hospital: 43, 58, 100
Horizon Photo Library: 101
The Hulton Deutsch Collection: 15, 33, 69, 86
ICM Artists: 54
Illinois Labor History Society: 82
Image Bank: 47, 67, 111, 117, 119
Indiana Historical Society Library: 84
Library of Congress: 79
National Aeronautics and Space Administration: 45, 57
National Archives: 6, 10, 11, 22, 29, 32, 74, 80
National Education Association: 48, 104, 109
National Institute of Standards and Technology, U.S. Department of Commerce: 37
National Oceanic and Atmospheric Administration: 56
National Portrait Gallery: 52
Kate Nunn: 118
Organization for Equal Education of the Sexes, Inc., © 1987: 97
Perkins School for the Blind: 91, 93
Paul Robertson: 110
Franklin D. Roosevelt Library: 88
Patrick Thomas: 115
UPI/Bettmann: 23, 25, 70, 72, 81, 96
U.S. Department of Justice: 39
Laura Waterman: 66
Women's Intercollegiate Athletics, University of Iowa: 60
Women Physicians Association Chartered: 59, 75

Index